National Emergency Communications Plan

July 2008

Homeland
Security

Message from the Secretary

Numerous after-action reports from major incidents throughout the history of emergency management in our Nation have cited communication difficulties among the many responding agencies as a major failing and challenge to policymakers. Congress and the Administration have recognized that a successful response to a future major incident—either a terrorist attack or natural disaster—requires a coordinated, "interoperable" response by the Nation's public safety, public health, and emergency management community, both public and private, at the Federal, State, tribal, Territorial, regional, and local levels.

Recognizing the need for an overarching strategy to help coordinate and guide such efforts, Congress directed the Department of Homeland Security to develop the first **National Emergency Communications Plan (NECP)**. The purpose of the NECP is to promote the ability of emergency response providers and relevant government officials to continue to communicate in the event of natural disasters, acts of terrorism, and other man-made disasters and to ensure, accelerate, and attain interoperable emergency communications nationwide.

Natural disasters and acts of terrorism have shown that there is no simple solution—or "silver bullet"—to solve the communications problems that still plague law enforcement, firefighting, rescue, and emergency medical personnel.

To strengthen emergency communications capabilities nationwide, the Plan focuses on technology, coordination, governance, planning, usage, training and exercises at all levels of government. This approach recognizes that communications operability is a critical building block for interoperability; emergency response officials first must be able to establish communications within their own agency before they can interoperate with neighboring jurisdictions and other agencies.

The NECP seeks to build on the substantial progress that we have made over the last several years. Among the key developments at the Federal, State, regional, and local levels are:

- Most Federal programs that support emergency communications have been consolidated within a single agency— **DHS**—to improve the alignment, integration, and coordination of the Federal mission.

- All 56 States and U.S. Territories have developed **Statewide Communication Interoperability Plans** (SCIP) that identify near- and long-term initiatives for improving communications interoperability.

- The Nation's **75 largest urban and metropolitan areas** maintain policies for interoperable communications.

- The **SAFECOM Interoperability Continuum** is widely accepted and used by the emergency response community to address critical elements for planning and implementing interoperability solutions. These elements include governance, standard operating procedures, technology, training and exercises, and usage of interoperable communications.
- The DHS Federal Emergency Management Agency (FEMA) is establishing **Regional Emergency Communications Coordination** (RECC) Working Groups in each of the 10 FEMA regions to coordinate multi-state efforts and measure progress on improving the survivability, sustainability, and interoperability of communications at the regional level.

In developing the NECP, DHS worked closely with stakeholders from all levels of government to ensure that their priorities and activities were addressed. The Department will continue to coordinate with Federal, State, local, and tribal governments, and the private sector, to ensure that the NECP is implemented successfully.

Ultimately, the NECP's goals cannot be achieved without the support and dedication of the emergency response community that was instrumental in crafting it. I ask everyone within the emergency response community to take ownership of the NECP's initiatives and actions and to dedicate themselves to meeting the key benchmarks. Working together, we can achieve our vision:

Emergency responders can communicate—
As needed, on demand, and as authorized;
At all levels of government; and
Across all disciplines.

Michael Chertoff
Secretary of Homeland Security

Table of Contents

Executive Summary ES-1

I. Introduction ....

1.1   Purpose of the National Emergency Communications Plan 1

1.2   Scope of the National Emergency Communications Plan 2

1.3   Organization of the NECP 5

II.   Defining the Future State of Emergency Communications 7

2.1   Vision 7

2.2   Goals 7

2.3   Capabilities Needed 8

III.   Achieving the Future State of Emergency Communications 10

Objective 1: Formal Governance Structures and Clear Leadership Roles 13

Objective 2: Coordinated Federal Activities 18

Objective 3: Common Planning and Operational Protocols 22

Objective 4: Standards and Emerging Communication Technologies 26

Objective 5: Emergency Responder Skills and Capabilities 30

Objective 6: System Life-Cycle Planning 33

Objective 7: Disaster Communications Capabilities 36

IV. Implementing and Measuring Achievement of the NECP 41

V. Conclusion 43

Executive Summary

Every day in cities and towns across the Nation, emergency response personnel respond to incidents of varying scope and magnitude. Their ability to communicate in real time is critical to establishing command and control at the scene of an emergency, to maintaining event situational awareness, and to operating overall within a broad range of incidents. As numerous after-action reports and national assessments[1] have revealed, however, there are still communications deficiencies that affect the ability of responders to manage routine incidents and support responses to natural disasters, acts of terrorism, and other incidents.

Recognizing the need for an overarching emergency communications strategy to address these shortfalls, Congress directed the Department of Homeland Security's (DHS) Office of Emergency Communications (OEC) to develop the first **National Emergency Communications Plan** (NECP). Title XVIII of the Homeland Security Act of 2002 (6 United States Code 101 et seq.), as amended, calls for the NECP to be developed in coordination with stakeholders from all levels of government and from the private sector.

In response, DHS worked with stakeholders from the Federal, State, local, and tribal levels to develop the NECP—a strategic plan that establishes a national vision for the future state of emergency communications. The desired future state is that **emergency responders can communicate:**
  - **As needed, on demand, and as authorized**
  - **At all levels of government**
  - **Across all disciplines.**

To measure progress toward this vision, three strategic goals were established:

Goal 1 — By 2010, 90 percent of all high-risk urban areas designated within the Urban Areas Security Initiative (UASI)[2] are able to demonstrate response-level emergency communications[3] within one hour for routine events involving multiple jurisdictions and agencies.

Goal 2 — By 2011, 75 percent of non-UASI jurisdictions are able to demonstrate response-level emergency communications within one hour for routine events involving multiple jurisdictions and agencies.

Goal 3 — By 2013, 75 percent of all jurisdictions are able to demonstrate response-level emergency communications within three hours, in the event of a significant incident as outlined in national planning scenarios.

---

[1] Examples include *The Federal Response to Hurricane Katrina: Lessons Learned*, February 2006; *The 9-11 Commission Report*, July 2004; and *The Final Report of the Select Bipartisan Committee to Investigate the Preparation for and Response to Hurricane Katrina*, February 2006.

[2] As identified in FY08 Homeland Security Grant Program or on the FEMA Grants website: http://www.fema.gov/pdf/government/grant/uasi/fy08_uasi_guidance.pdf.

[3] Response-level emergency communication refers to the capacity of individuals with primary operational leadership responsibility to manage resources and make timely decisions during an incident involving multiple agencies, without technical or procedural communications impediments.

To realize this national vision and meet these goals, the NECP established the following seven objectives for improving emergency communications for the Nation's Federal, State, local, and tribal emergency responders:

1. Formal decisionmaking structures and clearly defined leadership roles coordinate emergency communications capabilities.
2. Federal emergency communications programs and initiatives are collaborative across agencies and aligned to achieve national goals.
3. Emergency responders employ common planning and operational protocols to effectively use their resources and personnel.
4. Emerging technologies are integrated with current emergency communications capabilities through standards implementation, research and development, and testing and evaluation.
5. Emergency responders have shared approaches to training and exercises, improved technical expertise and enhanced response capabilities.
6. All levels of government drive long-term advancements in emergency communications through integrated strategic planning procedures, appropriate resource allocations, and public-private partnerships.
7. The Nation has integrated preparedness, mitigation, response, and recovery capabilities to communicate during significant events.

The NECP also provides recommended initiatives and milestones to guide emergency response providers and relevant government officials in making measurable improvements in emergency communications capabilities. The NECP recommendations help to guide, but not dictate, the distribution of homeland security funds to improve emergency communications at the Federal, State, and local levels and to support the implementation of the NECP.

Communications investments are some of the most significant, substantial, and long-lasting capital investments that agencies make; in addition, technological innovations for emergency communications are constantly evolving at a rapid pace. With these realities in mind, DHS recognizes that the emergency response community will, over time, realize this national vision in stages, as agencies invest in new communications systems and as new technologies emerge.

Further, DHS acknowledges there is no simple solution, or "silver bullet," for solving emergency communications challenges, and therefore has developed the NECP to make improvements at all levels of government in technology, coordination and governance, planning, usage, and training and exercises. This approach also recognizes that communications operability is a critical building block for interoperability: emergency response officials must first be able to establish communications within their own agency before they can interoperate with neighboring jurisdictions and other agencies.

Finally, DHS acknowledges that the Nation does not have unlimited resources to address deficiencies in emergency communications. For that reason, the NECP will be used to identify and prioritize investments to move the Nation toward this vision. As required by Congress, the NECP will be a living document subject to periodic review and updates by DHS in coordination with stakeholders. Future iterations will be revised based on progress made toward achieving the NECP's goals, on variations in national priorities, and on lessons learned from after-action reports.

I. Introduction

The ability of emergency responders to effectively communicate is paramount to the safety and security of our Nation. During the last three decades, the Nation has witnessed how inadequate emergency communications capabilities can adversely affect response and recovery efforts. Locally, agencies developed ad hoc solutions to overcome these challenges. The issue of inadequate coordination of emergency communications received national attention in the aftermath of the January 1982 passenger jet crash into the 14th Street Bridge (and, subsequently, the Potomac River) near downtown Washington, D.C; the inability of multiple jurisdictions to coordinate a response to the Air Florida crash began to drive regional collaboration. More recently, the terrorist attacks of September 11, Hurricane Katrina, and other natural and man-made disasters have demonstrated how emergency communications capabilities—including the lack of those capabilities— impact emergency responders, public health, national and economic security, and the ability of government leaders to maintain order and perform essential functions.[4]

During each of these events, the lack of coordinated emergency communications solutions and protocols among the responding agencies hindered response and recovery efforts. These events raised awareness of the issue among public policymakers and highlighted the critical role emergency communications plays in incident response. These events also prompted numerous national studies and assessments[5] on the state of emergency communications, which in turn has helped DHS to formulate a unified approach for addressing emergency communications.

1.1 Purpose of the National Emergency Communications Plan

The Homeland Security Act of 2002, as amended in 2006, mandated the creation of an overarching strategy to address emergency communications shortfalls. In addition, the emergency response community has sought national guidance to support a more integrated coordination of emergency communications priorities and investments. As a result, Congress directed the DHS' Office of

> **Purpose**
> - Set national goals and priorities for addressing deficiencies in the Nation's emergency communications posture
> - Provide recommendations and milestones for emergency response providers, relevant government officials, and Congress to improve emergency communications capabilitieS

---

[4] "Hurricane Katrina was the most destructive natural disaster in U.S. history. The storm crippled 38 911-call centers, disrupting local emergency services, and knocked out more than 3 million customer phone lines in Louisiana, Mississippi, and Alabama. Broadcast communications were likewise severely affected, as 50 percent of area radio stations and 44 percent of area television stations went off the air." White House Report, *The Federal Response to Katrina: Lessons Learned*, February 2006.

[5] Such as the *Final Report of the National Commission of Terrorist Attacks Upon the United States*, December 2001; the White House Report, *The Federal Response to Katrina: Lessons Learned*, February 2006; and the *Independent Panel Reviewing the Impact of Hurricane Katrina on Communications Networks—Report and Recommendations to the Federal Communications Commission*, June 12, 2006, all of which documented the numerous failures in emergency communications among emergency responders, which affected their ability to effectively respond to these incidents.

Emergency Communications (OEC)[6] to develop a plan to:

- Identify the capabilities needed by emergency responders to ensure the availability and interoperability of communications during emergencies, and identify obstacles to the deployment of interoperable communications systems
- Recommend both short- and long-term solutions for ensuring interoperability and continuity of communications for emergency responders, including recommendations for improving coordination among Federal, State, local, and tribal governments
- Set goals and timeframes for the deployment of interoperable emergency communications systems, and recommend measures that emergency response providers should employ to ensure the continued operation of communications infrastructure
- Set dates by which Federal agencies and State, local, and tribal governments expect to achieve a baseline level of national interoperable communications, and establish benchmarks to measure progress
- Guide the coordination of existing Federal emergency communications programs.[7]

1.2   Scope of the National Emergency Communications Plan

The National Emergency Communications Plan (NECP) focuses on the emergency communications needs of response personnel in every discipline, at every level of government and for the private sector and non-governmental organizations (NGO). **Emergency communications** is defined as the ability of emergency responders to exchange information via data, voice, and video as authorized, to complete their mission. Emergency response agencies at all levels of government must have interoperable and seamless communications to manage emergency response, establish command and control, maintain situational awareness, and function under a common operating picture, for a broad scale of incidents. Emergency communications consists of three primary elements:

1. **Operability**—The ability of emergency responders to establish and sustain communications in support of mission operations.

2. **Interoperability**—The ability of emergency responders to communicate among jurisdictions, disciplines, and levels of government, using a variety of frequency bands, as needed and as authorized. System operability is required for system interoperability.

3. **Continuity of Communications**—The ability of emergency response agencies to maintain communications in the event of damage to or destruction of the primary infrastructure.

---

[6] The OEC supports the Secretary of Homeland Security in developing, implementing, and coordinating interoperable and operable communications for the emergency response community at all levels of government. The OEC was directed by Title XVIII of the Homeland Security Act of 2002, as amended, to lead the development of a National Emergency Communications Plan.

[7] Appendix 4 provides more detailed information on DHS programs supporting emergency communications.

1.2.1   Approach to Developing the NECP

The majority of emergency incidents occur at the local level. Therefore, improving emergency communications—specifically, operability, interoperability, and continuity of communications—cannot be accomplished by the Federal Government alone. For this reason, DHS, through OEC, used a stakeholder-driven approach[8] in developing the NECP, one that included representatives from the Federal, State, and local responder communities as well as from the private sector. Exhibit 1 lists the partnerships and groups that provided input to the NECP.

Exhibit 1: Key Homeland Security and Emergency Communications Partnerships

Entity	Roles and Responsibilities
SAFECOM Executive Committee (EC) and Emergency Response Council (ERC)	The **SAFECOM EC** serves as the leadership group of the ERC and as the SAFECOM program's primary resource to access public safety practitioners and policymakers. The EC provides strategic leadership and guidance to the SAFECOM program on emergency-responder user needs and builds relationships with the ERC to leverage the ERC subject matter expertise. The **SAFECOM ERC** is a vehicle to provide a broad base of input from the of public safety community on its user needs to the SAFECOM program. The ERC provides a forum for individuals with specialized skills and common interests to share best practices and lessons learned so that interested parties at all levels of government can gain from one another's experience. Emergency responders and policymakers from Federal, State, local, and tribal governments comprise the SAFECOM EC and ERC.
Emergency Communications Preparedness Center (ECPC)	The ECPC was created under the authority of Title XVIII of the Homeland Security Act of 2002, as amended in 2006, to serve as the focal point and clearinghouse for intergovernmental information on interoperable emergency communications. The ECPC is an interdepartmental organization, currently composed of 12 Federal departments and agencies, to assess and coordinate Federal emergency communications operability and interoperability assurance efforts. The ECPC is the focal point for interagency emergency communications efforts and seeks to minimize the duplication of similar activities within the Federal Government. It also acts as an information clearinghouse to promote operable and interoperable communications in an all-hazards environment.
Federal Partnership for Interoperable Communications (FPIC)	The FPIC is a coordinating body that focuses on technical and operational matters within the Federal wireless communications community. Its mission is to address Federal wireless communications interoperability by fostering intergovernmental cooperation and by identifying and leveraging common synergies. The FPIC represents more than 40 Federal entities; its membership includes program managers of wireless systems, radio communications managers, Information Technology (IT) and Land Mobile Radio (LMR) specialists, and telecommunications engineers. State and local emergency responders participate as advisory members.
Project 25 Interface Committee (APIC)	As part of the Project 25 (P25) standards development process, the **Telecommunications Industry Association (TIA)** developed the APIC to resolve issues that arose during that process. The APIC is composed of private sector representatives and emergency response officials and serves as a liaison to facilitate user community and private sector relationships regarding the evolution and use of P25 standards.
National Public Safety Telecommunications Council (NPSTC)	The NPSTC is a federation of national public safety leadership organizations dedicated to improving emergency response communications and interoperability through collaborative leadership. The NPSTC is composed of State and local public safety representatives. In addition, Federal, Canadian, and other emergency communications partner organizations serve as liaisons to the NPSTC.

---

[8] Appendix 6 details the three-phased approach to develop the NECP that relied on stakeholder involvement.

Entity	Roles and Responsibilities
National Security Telecommunications Advisory Committee (NSTAC)	The NSTAC is composed of 30 private sector executives who represent major communications and network service providers as well as IT, finance, and aerospace companies. The NSTAC, through the National Communications System (NCS), provides private sector-based analyses and recommendations to the President and the Executive Branch on policy and enhancements to national security and emergency preparedness (NS/EP) communications.
Critical Infrastructure Partnership Advisory Council (CIPAC)	The CIPAC is a DHS program established to facilitate effective coordination between government infrastructure protection programs and the infrastructure protection activities of the owners and operators of critical infrastructure and key resources. The CIPAC enables public and private sector representatives to engage in candid, substantive discussions regarding the protection of the Nation's critical infrastructure.

The NECP has been designed to complement and support overarching homeland security and emergency communications legislation, strategies, and initiatives. The NECP applies guidance from these authorities, including key principles and priorities, to establish the first national strategic plan that is focused exclusively on improving emergency communications for emergency response providers nationwide. As demonstrated in Exhibit 2 below, the NECP provides a critical link between national communications priorities and strategic and tactical planning at the regional, State, and local levels. Appendix 2 provides a comprehensive listing and explanation of these documents.

Exhibit 2: Key Homeland Security and Emergency Communications Authorities

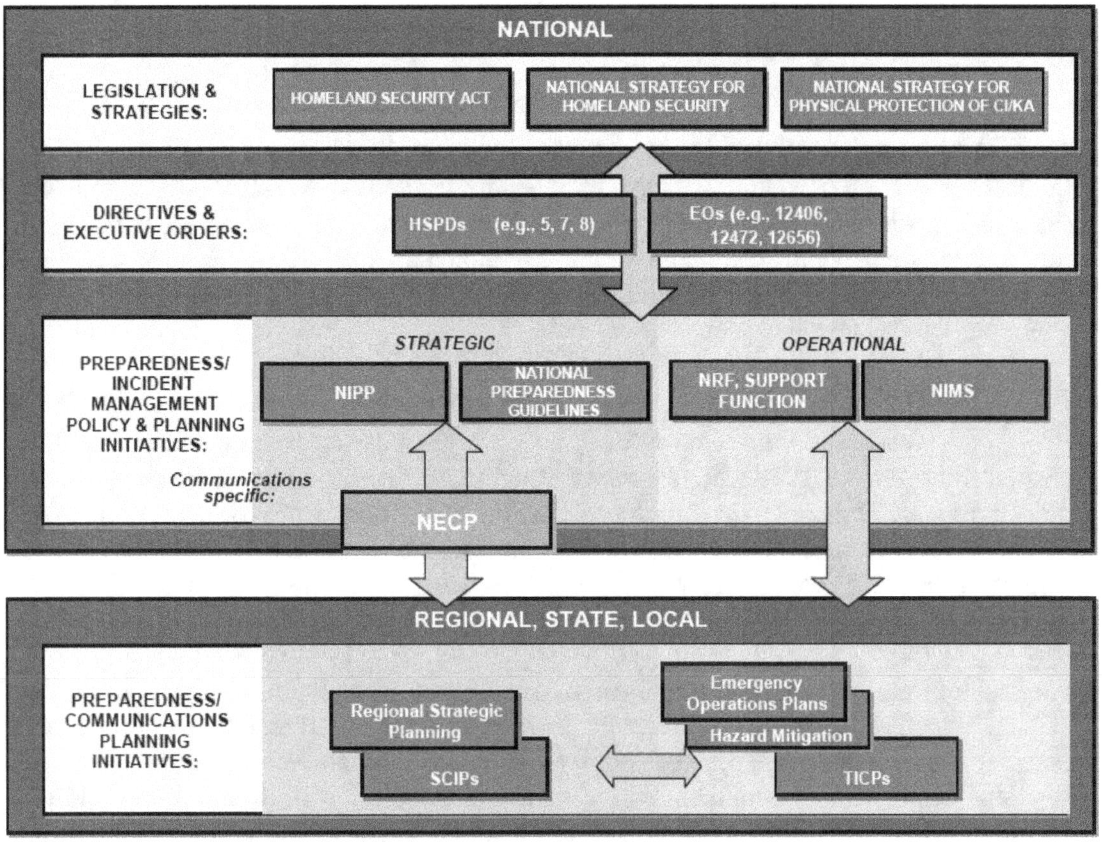

1.3   Organization of the NECP

The NECP establishes a national vision for the desired future state of emergency communications. It sets strategic goals, national objectives, and supporting initiatives to drive the Nation toward that future state. The NECP also provides recommended milestones to guide emergency response providers and relevant government officials as they make measurable improvements to their emergency communications capabilities.

As illustrated in Exhibit 3, three logical steps comprise the NECP approach and inform the organization of this document: 1) defining the future state of emergency communications; 2) developing a strategy to achieve the future state; and 3) implementing the future state and measuring how well it is being implemented.

Exhibit 3: NECP Approach and Organization

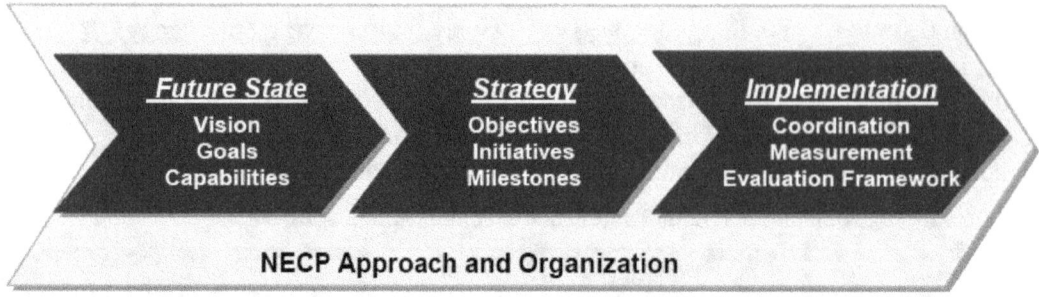

1.3.1   Defining the Future State of Emergency Communications

In this first step, DHS worked with stakeholders to develop an overall **Vision** statement (Section 2.1) and established three high-level **Goals** (Section 2.2) that define the desired future state of emergency communications. DHS then identified the emergency communications **Capabilities Needed** (Section 2.3) for the emergency response community to achieve the desired future state.

1.3.2   Developing a Strategy to Achieve the Future State

Based on the capabilities needed for the emergency response community to achieve the desired future state, DHS developed seven **Objectives** (Section III). Although all seven objectives were designed to lead to the realization of the long-term vision, execution of all initiatives and achievement of national milestones are not necessarily prerequisites for achieving the three goals. DHS will continue to work with its stakeholders on the implementation of the NECP initiatives and the attainment of these near-term goals.

For each objective, DHS developed **Supporting Initiatives** (Section III), with a focus on driving outcomes toward the future state. In crafting each initiative, DHS identified both relevant and current emergency communications activities that affect the initiative and key gaps that drive action in the initiative area. Finally, DHS identified **Recommended National Milestones** (Section III) that detail the timeline and outcomes of each initiative.

1.3.3   Implementing and Measuring Achievement of the Future State

In the final step, DHS provides guidance for implementing the NECP and recommendations for measuring success (Section IV). These recommendations are based on the legislative requirements for the NECP as outlined in Appendix 1.

II.   Defining the Future State of Emergency Communications

The NECP outlines the future vision of emergency communications over the next five years. In doing so, it establishes tangible goals by which success can be measured.

2.1   Vision

The NECP vision is to ensure operability, interoperability, and continuity of communications to allow emergency responders to communicate as needed, on demand, and as authorized at all levels of government and across all disciplines.

> **Vision**
>
> *Emergency response personnel can communicate—*
>
> - *As needed, on demand, and as authorized*
> - *At all levels of government*
> - *Across all disciplines*

2.2   Goals

To work toward this desired future state, DHS defined a series of goals that establish a minimum level of interoperable communications and dates by which Federal, State, local, and tribal agencies are expected to achieve that minimum level. Although not comprehensive, these goals provide an initial set of operational targets that will be further expanded by OEC through a process that engages Federal, State, and local governments, the private sector, and emergency responders. Section 4.2 outlines how OEC plans to measure the nationwide achievement of these goals.

Emergency responders who train regularly and who use emergency communications solutions daily are able to use emergency communications more effectively during major incidents; therefore, the first two goals focus on day-to-day response capabilities that will inherently enhance emergency response capabilities.

Response-level emergency communications is the capacity of individuals with primary operational leadership responsibility to manage resources and make timely decisions during an incident involving multiple agencies, without technical or procedural communications impediments.[9] In addition to communicating to first-level subordinates in the field, an Operations Section Chief should be able to communicate upward to the incident command level (i.e., between the Operations Section Chief and Incident Command).[10] As an incident grows and transitions, Incident Command/Unified Command may move off-scene, which may require establishing communications between Incident Command and off-scene Emergency Operations Centers (EOC), dispatch centers, and other support groups as appropriate.

---

[9] As defined in the National Incident Command System 200, Unit 2: "Leadership and Management."

[10] As defined in the National Incident Management System, FEMA 501/Draft August 2007, p.47.

Goal 1—By 2010, 90 percent of all high-risk urban areas designated within the Urban Areas Security Initiative (UASI)[11] are able to demonstrate response-level emergency communications within one hour for routine events[12] involving multiple jurisdictions[13] and agencies.

Goal 2—By 2011, 75 percent of non-UASI jurisdictions are able to demonstrate response-level emergency communications within one hour for routine events involving multiple jurisdictions and agencies.

Goal 3—By 2013, 75 percent of all jurisdictions are able to demonstrate response-level emergency communications within three hours, in the event of a significant event[14] as outlined in national planning scenarios.

The NECP identifies seven key objectives to move the Nation toward its overall vision. Although all seven objectives are important to achieving all three goals, Objective 7 primarily focuses on enhancing the ability to communicate during a significant event as outlined in Goal 3. Further, DHS, through OEC and the Federal Emergency Management Agency's (FEMA) Regional Emergency Communications Coordination Working Groups (RECCWG), will collaborate with State homeland security directors and State interoperability coordinators to develop appropriate methodologies to measure progress toward these goals in each State.

2.3   Capabilities Needed

Leveraging the findings from various sources of information, including analyses, from Federal, State, local, and tribal governments on emergency communications, DHS completed a comprehensive examination of emergency communications capabilities across all levels of government and some private sector entities.[15] (A **capability** enables the accomplishment of a mission or task.) Exhibit 4 summarizes the range of emergency communications capabilities needed by emergency responders and maps those to the **SAFECOM Interoperability Continuum**.[16] These identified capabilities serve as the

---

[11] As identified in the FY08 Homeland Security Grant Program or on the FEMA Grants website: http://www.fema.gov/pdf/government/grant/uasi/fy08_uasi_guidance.pdf.

[12] Routine events—During routine events, the emphasis for response-level emergency communications is on operability and interoperability. These types of events are further delineated in the Usage element of the SAFECOM Interoperability Continuum as planned events, localized emergency incidents, regional incident management (interstate or intrastate), and daily use throughout the region. See Appendix 5 for a further description of the SAFECOM Interoperability Continuum.

[13] Jurisdiction—A geographical, political, or system boundary as defined by each individual State.

[14] Significant events—During significant events, the emphasis for response-level emergency communications is on interoperability and continuity of communications. Homeland Security Presidential Directive 8: National Preparedness (HSPD-8) sets forth 15 National Planning Scenarios, highlighting a plausible range of significant events such as terrorist attacks, major disasters, and other emergencies that pose the greatest risks to the Nation. Any of these 15 scenarios should be considered when planning for a significant event during which all major emergency communications infrastructure is destroyed.

[15] The *National Communications Capabilities Report*, 2008.

[16] SAFECOM's Interoperability Continuum was designed to help the emergency response community and local, tribal, state, and Federal policymakers address critical elements for success as they plan and implement interoperability solutions: http://www.safecomprogram.gov/SAFECOM/tools/continuum/default.html.

foundation for the NECP priority objectives, initiatives, and recommended national milestones set forth in Section III.

Exhibit 4: Emergency Communications Capabilities Needed to Achieve Future State

Lanes of the SAFECOM Interoperability Continuum	Capabilities Needed
Governance	• Strong government leadership • Formal, thorough, and inclusive interagency governance structures • Clear lines of communication and decision-making • Strategic planning processes
Standard Operating Procedures (SOP)	• Standardized and uniform emergency responder interaction during emergency response operations • Standardized use and application of interoperable emergency communications terminology, solutions, and backup systems
Technology	• Voice and data standards that pertain to real-time situational information exchange and reports for emergency responders before, during, and after response • Uniform model and standard for emergency data information exchange • Testing and evaluation of emergency communications technology to help agencies make informed decisions about technology • Emergency response communications technology based on voluntary consensus standards • Basic level of communications systems operability
Training and Exercises	• Uniform, standardized performance objectives to measure effectiveness of emergency responders communications capabilities • Emergency response providers who are fully knowledgeable, trained, and exercised on the use and application of day-to-day and backup communications equipment, systems, and operations irrespective of the size of the emergency response
Usage	• Adequate resources and planning to cover not only initial system and equipment investment but for the entire life cycle (operations, exercising, and maintenance) • Broad regional (interstate and intrastate) coordination in technology investment and procurement planning

III.   Achieving the Future State of Emergency Communications

This section describes the strategy for achieving the NECP's future state for emergency communications and for meeting the overall goals identified in Section II. Specifically, this section discusses in detail the seven **Objectives** that delineate a comprehensive assessment of the capabilities needed to close existing gaps and achieve the long-term vision. In the near- term, DHS will continue to work with its stakeholders on the implementation of the NECP initiatives and the attainment of near-term goals. As previously defined, the three critical elements of emergency communications are operability, interoperability, and continuity of communications. Progress toward achieving each of the seven objectives is essential in realizing improvements in all three of these primary elements to emergency communications.[17]

In addition, this section defines **Supporting Initiatives** for each objective, with a focus on driving outcomes toward the future state. Each initiative identifies current emergency communications activities and key gaps in the initiative area. Finally, **National Milestones** are recommended that detail the timelines and outcomes of each initiative.

3.1 Objectives, Initiatives, and Milestones

The objectives and initiatives provide national guidance to Federal, State, local, and tribal agencies to implement key activities to improve emergency communications. Milestones provide key checkpoints to monitor the implementation of the NECP. The milestones' timelines begin when the NECP is released. The proposed timelines for completing these initiatives begin upon delivery of the NECP to Congress. OEC will then coordinate with partner organizations at all levels of government and with nongovernmental associations and private sector organizations, to develop implementation strategies.

The NECP identifies the following objectives to improve emergency communications for Federal, State, local, and tribal emergency responders across the Nation:

1. Formal decisionmaking structures and clearly defined leadership roles coordinate emergency communications capabilities.
2. Federal emergency communications programs and initiatives are collaborative across agencies and aligned to achieve national goals.
3. Emergency responders employ common planning and operational protocols to effectively use their resources and personnel.
4. Emerging technologies are integrated with current emergency communications capabilities through standards implementation, research and development, and testing and evaluation.
5. Emergency responders have shared approaches to training and exercises, improved technical expertise, and enhanced response capabilities.

---

[17] Note that the objectives are not solely relevant or categorized against operability, interoperability, or continuity of communications. Rather, progress in each objective area will result in improvements in each of the three emergency communications components.

6. All levels of government drive long-term advancements in emergency communications through integrated strategic planning procedures, appropriate resource allocations, and public-private partnerships.
7. The Nation has integrated preparedness, mitigation, response, and recovery capabilities to communicate during significant events.

Significant levels of cooperation and collaboration across the stakeholder community are necessary to achieve all of the milestones in each objective. The supporting initiatives and recommended national milestones represent the DHS' position on actions that must occur, and establish completion dates to meet NECP goals. DHS continues to work with stakeholders at all levels of government to identify and verify ownership roles to drive full participation and implementation of this Plan.

For some of the milestones, specific leadership and ownership roles are identified based on relevant mission areas, current activities, existing authorities, and feedback from organizations during NECP development. In many cases, specific leadership roles to achieve the milestones are not and presently cannot be identified; although DHS has been mandated by Congress to develop the NECP and coordinate its implementation, DHS has limited authority to compel responsibilities and leadership roles—and the associated expenditure of resources—for external organizations. To implement the NECP, OEC will collaborate with its partner organizations to develop strategies that guide achievement of the objectives, initiatives, and milestones.

Exhibit 4 on the following page illustrates these integrated elements of the NECP, which includes a vision of the future state and overall goals that support the achievement of the vision; specific objectives to meet these goals; and supporting initiatives with national milestones that define the outcomes and timelines required.

Exhibit 4: The NECP Roadmap

EMERGENCY RESPONSE PERSONNEL CAN COMMUNICATE

- All levels of government
- All disciplines
- As needed, on demand, and as authorized

Goal 1 – By 2010, 90 percent of all high risk urban areas designated within the Urban Area Security Initiative (UASI) are able to demonstrate response-level emergency communications within one hour for routine events involving multiple jurisdictions and agencies.

Goal 2 – By 2011, 75 percent of non-UASI jurisdictions are able to demonstrate response-level emergency communications within one hour for routine events involving multiple jurisdictions and agencies.

Goal 3 – By 2013, 75 percent of all jurisdictions are able to demonstrate response-level emergency communications within three hours, in the event of a significant incident as outlined in national planning scenarios.

	Formal Governance Structures and Clear Leadership Roles	Coordinated Federal Activities	Common Planning and Operational Protocols	Standards and Emerging Communication Technologies	Emergency Responder Skills and Capabilities	System Life-Cycle Planning	Disaster Communications Capabilities
INITIATIVES	**Initiative 1.1** Facilitate the development of effective governance groups and designated emergency communications leadership roles. **Initiative 1.2** Develop standardized emergency communications performance objectives and link to DHS' overall system for assessing preparedness capabilities nationwide. **Initiative 1.3** Integrate strategic and tactical emergency communications planning efforts across all levels of government. **Initiative 1.4** Develop coordinated grant policies that promote Federal participation and coordination in communications planning processes, governance bodies, joint training and exercises, and infrastructure sharing.	**Initiative 2.1** Establish a source of information about Federal emergency communications programs and initiatives. **Initiative 2.2** Coordinate all technical assistance programs to provide greater consistency for the delivery of Federal services. **Initiative 2.3** Target Federal emergency communications grants to address gaps identified in the NECP, SCIPs and TICPs. **Initiative 2.4** Enable resource sharing and improve operational efficiencies. **Initiative 2.5** Establish interoperability capabilities and coordination between domestic and international partners.	**Initiative 3.1** Standardize and implement common operational protocols and procedures. **Initiative 3.2** Implementation of the NIMS and the NRF across all levels of government. **Initiative 3.3** Develop and implement model SOPs for specific events, and all-hazards response.	**Initiative 4.1** Adopt voluntary consensus standards for voice and data emergency response capabilities. **Initiative 4.2** Research, develop, test, and evaluate new voice, video, and data solutions for emergency communications based on user-driven needs and requirements. **Initiative 4.3** Transition to and/or integrate legacy systems with next-generation technologies based on voluntary consensus standards. **Initiative 4.4** Implement the Advanced Encryption Standard (AES) for Federal responders.	**Initiative 5.1** Develop and implement national training programs and certification processes. **Initiative 5.2** Develop and inject standardized emergency communications performance objectives and evaluation criteria into operational exercises. **Initiative 5.3** Provide targeted training to improve skills and capabilities of technical staff.	**Initiative 6.1** Conduct system life-cycle planning to better forecast long-term funding requirements. **Initiative 6.2** Expand the use of public and private sector partnerships related to emergency communications. **Initiative 6.3** Assess existing Federal mission-critical wireless capabilities and upgrade and modernize them according to mission needs. **Initiative 6.4** Enhance emergency communications system survivability using redundant and resilient system designs.	**Initiative 7.1** Provide an integration framework for disaster communications operations and response to ensure that the Federal Government can effectively fulfill requests during incident response. **Initiative 7.2** Implement disaster communications planning and preparedness activities. **Initiative 7.3** Leverage existing and emerging technologies to expand and integrate disaster communications capabilities among emergency response providers. **Initiative 7.4** Accelerate the implementation of emergency communications components in the NRF, specifically national access and credentialing. **Initiative 7.5** Implement systems and procedures that ensure the Federal Government's ability to establish situational awareness, develop a common operating picture, and provide timely and consistent information during crises. **Initiative 7.6** Promote the use of and expand the capabilities of priority services programs (e.g., GETS, WPS, TSP) to next generation networks.

Objective 1: Formal Governance Structures and Clear Leadership Roles

Formal decision-making structures and clearly defined leadership roles coordinate emergency communications capabilities.

More than 50,000 independent agencies across the Nation routinely use emergency communications, and each of these agencies is governed by the laws of its respective jurisdiction or area of responsibility. No single entity is, or can be, in charge of the Nation's entire emergency communications infrastructure. In such an environment, collaborative planning among all levels of government is critical for ensuring effective and fully coordinated preparedness and response. Formal governance structures and leadership are needed to manage these complex systems of people, organizations, and technologies.[18]

Current Emergency Communications Activities:[19]
- National-level policies (e.g., National Response Framework [NRF] and its Emergency Support Function #2 [ESF#2], National Incident Management System [NIMS] Joint Field Office Activation and Operations—Interagency Integrated Standard Operating Procedure Annex E) identify roles, responsibilities, and coordinating structures for incident management.
- The Statewide Communication Interoperability Plan (SCIP) Guidebook provides guidance on establishing a structure for governing statewide communications interoperability planning efforts. All 56 States and territories now have SCIPs.
- The ECPC establishes a governance and decision-making structure for strategic coordination of interdepartmental emergency communications at the Federal level.
- FEMA leads the integration of tactical Federal emergency communications during disasters and is developing requirements and an associated Disaster Emergency Communications (DEC) Integration Framework for fulfilling emergency communications needs during disasters.
- Decision-making bodies at the State, regional, and local levels (e.g., RECCWG,[20] statewide interoperability coordinators and executive committees, local communications committees) coordinate emergency communications issues.

---

[18] Most emergency response events occur at the local level and are managed by local incident commanders. To best support the local incident commander, Federal and State agencies must ensure the coordination of their interoperability efforts with local agencies. This perspective is in agreement with the ERC's guiding principles, *SAFECOM Emergency Response Council, Agreements on a Nationwide Plan for Interoperable Communications, Summer 2007.*

[19] A subset of relevant and current emergency communication activities has been identified for each objective in the NECP; these subsets are not meant to be comprehensive, but represent examples of stakeholder input collected during NECP development. Many additional activities are planned and underway across all levels of government.

[20] As defined in Section 1805 of the Department of Homeland Security Act of 2007, RECCWGs assess emergency communications capabilities within their respective regions, facilitate disaster preparedness through the promotion of multijurisdictional and multiagency emergency communications networks, and ensure activities are coordinated with all emergency communications stakeholders within the RECCWG's specific FEMA region. The FEMA Regional Administrator oversees the RECCWG and its activities, and the RECCWG is required to report annually (at a minimum) to the FEMA Regional Administrator. The RECCWG advises on all aspects of emergency communications in its respective Region and incorporates input from emergency communications stakeholders and representatives from all levels of government as well as from nongovernmental and private sector agencies.

- OEC is developing a governance sustainability and SCIP implementation methodology to provide guidance and lessons learned in creating and sustaining effective statewide communications interoperability governance structures for SCIP implementation.

Key Gaps and Obstacles Driving Action:
- In many cases, emergency response agencies are unaware of or have yet to adopt and integrate national-level policies that identify roles, responsibilities, and coordinating structures for emergency communications.
- State Interoperability Executive Committees (SIECs) or their equivalents do not have uniform structures, act in an ad hoc capacity, and often lack inclusive membership.
- The Nation does not have an objective, standardized framework to identify and assess emergency communications capabilities nationwide. Thus, it is difficult for jurisdictions to invest in building and maintaining appropriate levels of operability, interoperability, and continuity of communications.
- Emergency communications strategic planning efforts vary in scope and often do not address the operability and interoperability concerns of all relevant stakeholders.
- Many agencies often do not consider communications planning to be a priority and therefore do not allocate resources for participation in planning activities.
- There is a need for greater Federal department and agency participation in State, regional, and local governance and planning processes.
- Many States do not have full-time statewide interoperability coordinators, or equivalent positions, to focus on the activities needed to drive change.

Supporting Initiatives and Milestones to Address Key Gaps:
- **Initiative 1.1: Facilitate the development of effective governance groups and designated emergency communications leadership roles.** Uniform criteria and best practices for governance and emergency communications leadership across the Nation will better equip emergency response agencies to make informed decisions that meet the needs of their communities. Establishing effective leadership positions and representative governance groups nationwide will standardize decision-making and enhance the ability of emergency response agencies to share information and respond to incidents.

  ### Recommended National Milestones:
  - Within 12 months, DHS will establish a central repository of model formal agreements (i.e., Memorandums of Agreement [MOAs], Memorandums of Understanding [MOUs], and Mission Assignments) and information that will enhance interstate and intrastate coordination.[21]
  - Within 12 months, all States and Territories should establish full-time statewide interoperability coordinators or equivalent positions.
  - Within 12 months, DHS will conduct a National Emergency Communications workshop to provide an opportunity for RECCWG

---

[21] This repository is envisioned as a component of the ECPC clearinghouse function. Please refer to Initiative 2.1 for additional information and activities regarding the ECPC clearinghouse.

participants, statewide emergency communications coordinators, and other interested parties to collaborate with one another and with Federal representatives from the ECPC and FPIC.

o   Within 12 months, RECCWGs are fully established as a primary link for disaster emergency communications among all levels of government at the FEMA regional level, sharing information, identifying common problems, and coordinating multistate operable and interoperable emergency response initiatives and plans among Federal, State, local, and tribal agencies.[22]

o   Within 12 months, SIECs (or their equivalents) in all 56 States and Territories should incorporate the recommended membership as outlined in the SCIP Guidebook and should be established via legislation or executive order by an individual State's governor.

o   Within 18 months, DHS will publish uniform criteria and best practices for establishing governance groups and emergency communications leadership roles across the Nation.

- **Initiative 1.2: Develop standardized emergency communications performance objectives and link to DHS' overall system for assessing preparedness capabilities nationwide.** DHS will collaborate with Federal, regional, State,[23] local, and tribal governments and organizations, as well as with the private sector, to develop a more comprehensive and targeted set of evaluation criteria for defining and measuring communications requirements across the Nation. DHS will ensure these assessment efforts leverage existing reporting requirements (e.g., for SCIPs, Tactical Interoperable Communications Plans [TICPs], and State Preparedness Reports) and grant program applications (e.g., for the Interoperable Emergency Communications Grant Program [IECGP] and the Homeland Security Grant Program [HSGP]) to prevent duplicative reporting requirements for its stakeholders. Evaluation criteria will be based on the approach being followed in DHS' implementation plans for the National Preparedness Guidelines/Target Capabilities List (TCL).[24]

---

[22] FEMA organizes the United States into 10 FEMA regions. Each FEMA region has its own Regional Headquarters led by a Regional Administrator. FEMA regions are responsible for working in partnership with emergency management agencies from each state within the respective region to prepare for, respond to, and recover from disasters. FEMA regions and their Regional Administrators will be leveraged to provide oversight, implementation, and execution for their respective RECCWGs.

[23] This collaboration would include State homeland security advisors and statewide interoperability coordinators.

[24] DHS is currently developing TCL implementation plans for animal health, EOC management, intelligence, onsite incident management, mass transit protection, and weapons of mass destruction (WMD)/hazardous material (hazmat) rescue and decontamination. Communication requirements will be based on the concepts and principles outlined in the NECP and in the baseline principles provided in the NIMS (e.g., common operating picture; interoperability; reliability, scalability and portability; and resiliency and redundancy). These requirements will be built on the command requirements for response-level emergency communications as defined in the NECP, and will also include the full range of communications requirements for all of the standardized types of communications (e.g., strategic, tactical, support, public address) identified in the NIMS.

Recommended National Milestones:
- o Within 12 months, DHS will develop a standardized framework for identifying and assessing emergency communications capabilities nationwide.
- o Within 18 months, DHS' emergency communications capability framework, in preparation for release, will be reviewed during a series of technical working group meetings with stakeholders from the emergency response community.
- o Within 24 months, the emergency communications capability framework will be incorporated as the communications and information management capability in the DHS/FEMA National Preparedness Guidelines/TCL, which will serve as a basis for future grant policies.

- **Initiative 1.3: Integrate strategic and tactical emergency communications planning efforts across all levels of government.** Tactical and strategic coordination will eliminate unnecessary duplication of effort and maximize interagency synchronization, bringing together tactical response and strategic planning.

Recommended National Milestones:
- o Within 12 months, DHS will make available an effective communications-asset management tool containing appropriate security and privacy controls to allow for nationwide intergovernmental use.
- o Within 12 months, tactical planning among Federal, State, local, and tribal governments occurs at the regional interstate level.

- **Initiative 1.4: Develop coordinated grant policies that promote Federal participation and coordination in communications planning processes, governance bodies, joint training and exercises, and infrastructure sharing.** The largest investment category of DHS grant funds is interoperable communications. Federal acquisition, deployment, and operating funds supporting Federal mission-critical communication systems often cannot be used to support State and local communication needs (when otherwise appropriate). These limitations on the use of these funds can inhibit the realization of the goals of coordination and interoperability, as systems are developed, deployed, and maintained.

Recommended National Milestones:
- o Within 12 months, DHS fiscal year (FY) 2009 grant policies provides guidance on how to best support national interoperability needs through the promotion of shared infrastructure, cooperative planning, and coordinated governance.

      o Within 12 months, best practices for sharing infrastructure, addressing spectrum issues, and developing agreements among Federal, State, and local emergency response communicators are promoted through DHS technical assistance programs, in accordance with applicable laws.

Objective 2: Coordinated Federal Activities

Federal emergency communications programs and initiatives are collaborative across agencies and aligned to achieve national goals.

Federal departments and agencies rely on emergency communications capabilities to support mission-critical operations (e.g., law enforcement, disaster response, homeland security). Traditionally, Federal departments and agencies have not considered the benefits of planning and implementing emergency communications systems in conjunction with Federal, State, and local agencies. It is critical that Federal programs and initiatives—including grant programs—responsible for managing and providing emergency communications, are coordinated to minimize duplication, maximize Federal investments, and ensure interoperability.

Current Emergency Communications Activities:
- The ECPC has been established to serve as the Federal focal point for interoperable emergency communications. An ECPC clearinghouse is being designed as a central repository for Federal, State, local, and tribal governments to publish and share tactics, techniques, practices, programs, and policies that enhance interoperability for emergency communications.
- RECCWGs are being established to provide regional coordination points for emergency communications preparedness, response, and recovery for Federal, State, local, and tribal governments within each FEMA region.
- Federal, State, and local agencies are both independently and jointly upgrading and modernizing their tactical communications systems. There are several Federal grant programs (e.g., the HSGP and the Public Safety Interoperable Communications [PSIC] Grant Program) that State, local, and tribal entities can use to enhance their emergency communications capabilities.
- DHS is establishing the IECGP to support projects that focus on improving operable and interoperable emergency communications for State, local, and tribal agencies and for international border agencies. IECGP guidance is being developed to close gaps associated with governance, planning, training, and exercises and currently focuses grant funds on initiatives that are not focused on technology.
- OEC's Interoperable Communications Technical Assistance Program (ICTAP) helps to enhance interoperable emergency communications among Federal, State, local, and tribal governments by providing assistance on governance, SOPs, technology, training and exercises, usage, and engineering issues. The ICTAP leverages and works with other Federal, State, and local interoperability efforts whenever possible to enhance the overall capacity for agencies and individuals to communicate with one another.

Key Gaps and Obstacles Driving Action:
- Information on Federal emergency communications programs, activities, and standards is not consistently or adequately shared with State and local agencies.
- Federal emergency responders are not integrated into existing State and local networks because of capacity, frequency coordination, and channel congestion issues.

- Federal grant programs for interoperable emergency communications are not targeting gaps in a consistent and coordinated manner.
- There is a lack of overall Federal coordination at the regional level and participation in regional UASI and statewide planning activities (e.g., SIEC).
- Regulatory and legal issues act as barriers to the further use of shared capabilities across all levels of government.

Supporting Initiatives and Milestones to Address Key Gaps:
- **Initiative 2.1: Establish a source of information about Federal emergency communications programs and initiatives.** There are a number of Federal programs and initiatives focused on emergency communications. DHS will establish a focal point for coordinating intergovernmental emergency communications to assist the Federal Government in identifying duplicative efforts and achieving greater economies of scale.

  Recommended National Milestones:
  - Within 12 months, Federal departments and agencies leverage the ECPC as the central coordinating body for providing Federal input into, and comments on, Federal emergency communications projects, plans, and reports.
  - Within 12 months and annually thereafter, the ECPC submits a strategic assessment to Congress, detailing both progress to date and the remaining obstacles to interoperable emergency communications and Federal coordination efforts.
  - Within 12 months, DHS establishes a uniform method for coordination and information sharing between ECPC and the RECCWGs.
  - Within 18 months, commence operation of the ECPC web-based clearinghouse portal, with strong consideration given to leveraging existing portals, such as the Homeland Security Information Network (HSIN), DHS ONE-Net, and DHS Interactive.
  - Within 24 months, DHS establishes targeted outreach and training activities to ensure that stakeholders across the Nation are aware of the availability of ECPC clearinghouse resources.

- **Initiative 2.2: Coordinate all technical assistance programs to provide greater consistency for the delivery of Federal services.** Coordinated and uniform technical assistance will improve the reliability of communications systems and operator expertise. Technical assistance can be targeted to address gaps identified in SCIPs and the priorities outlined in the NECP.

  Recommended National Milestones:
  - Within 6 months, through the ECPC, a catalog of current technical assistance programs will be established, to both ensure the availability of technical assistance and reduce duplication.
  - Within 6 months, DHS establishes a focal point for consistent and comprehensive technical assistance and guidance for emergency communications planning with Federal, State, local, and tribal agencies.

- o Within 12 months, Federal agencies establish a common methodology across all Federal operability and interoperability technical assistance programs and will train the personnel who provide technical assistance on the use of this methodology.
- o Within 18 months, DHS establishes a consistent and coordinated method for States and localities to request Federal technical assistance.

- **Initiative 2.3: Target Federal emergency communications grants to address gaps identified in the NECP, SCIPs, and TICPs**. Targeted Federal grants will allow emergency response agencies to address communications gaps and coordinate planning efforts. Federal grant funding represents only a small fraction of overall emergency response emergency communications investment. Although Federal grant funding is a small fraction of emergency communication investment, such funding is a key tool by which State and local emergency response agencies can address national emergency communication priorities.

  Recommended National Milestones:
  - o Within 12 months, all IECGP investments are coordinated with the statewide interoperability coordinator and SIEC, or its equivalent, to support State administrative agency investments including the filling of gaps as identified in the NECP and SCIPs.
  - o Within 12 months, DHS grant policies are developed to encourage regional operable and interoperable solutions, including shared solutions, and to prioritize cost-effective measures and multi-applicant investments.
  - o Within 12 months, the ECPC stands up a working group to coordinate grant priorities across Federal grant programs.

- **Initiative 2.4: Enable resource sharing and improve operational efficiencies.** Most government-owned wireless infrastructure that supports emergency response exists at the State and local levels. Further, many State and local agencies have or are in the process of modernizing and expanding their systems through mechanisms such as Federal grant programs (e.g., the HSGP and the PSIC Grant Program). By working with State and local agencies, Federal agencies can benefit from these improvements by leveraging both existing and planned infrastructure, where appropriate, to improve operability and interoperability. In addition, there are a number of Federal-level programs and initiatives involving the deployment of communications infrastructure, which present opportunities for resource and infrastructure sharing (e.g., spectrum, Radio Frequency [RF] sites). Federal agencies should work to better understand existing and planned programs, initiatives, and infrastructure across all levels of government to improve coordination, maximize investments, and more quickly field capabilities.

  Recommended National Milestones:
  - o Within 6 months, DHS conducts an assessment of shared regional/State systems, to determine the potential for resource sharing among Federal, State, local, and tribal agencies.

    o Within 12 months, DHS prioritizes sharing opportunities, based on Federal emergency communications requirements.

    o Within 24 months, DHS establishes partnerships between Federal, State, local, and tribal agencies, as appropriate.

- **Initiative 2.5: Establish interoperability capabilities and coordination between domestic and international partners**. Emergencies occurring near the Mexican and Canadian borders often require a bi-national response, necessitating interoperability with international partners. These countries often have different technical configurations and regulatory statutes than the United States. Coordination is essential to ensure that domestic and international legal and regulatory requirements are followed.

Recommended National Milestones:

    o Within 6 months, and annually thereafter, hold plenary meetings of the United States-Mexico Joint Commission on Resolution of Radio Interference to address identified interference cases between the United States and Mexico.

    o Within 12 months, DHS establishes best practices for emergency communications coordination with international partners (i.e., cross border interoperability coordination with Mexico and Canada).

    o Within 24 months, DHS establishes demonstration projects between Federal, State, local, and tribal agencies, and international partners, to improve interoperability in border areas that are at risk for large-scale incidents (natural or man-made) requiring international responses (including illegal border crossings or smuggling activities that result from an incident).

Objective 3: Common Planning and Operational Protocols

Emergency responders employ common planning and operational protocols to effectively use their resources and personnel.

Agencies often create SOPs to meet their unique emergency communications requirements. In recent years, with support from the Federal Government, emergency responders have developed standards for interoperability channel naming, the use of existing nationwide interoperability frequencies, and the use of plain language. NIMS represents an initial step in establishing national consistency for how agencies and jurisdictions define their operations; however, additional steps are required to continue streamlining response procedures.

Current Emergency Communications Activities:
- National-level preparedness and incident management doctrines (e.g., NRF, NIMS, Joint Field Office Activation and Operations Interagency Integrated Standard Operating Procedures, TCLs) are in various stages of development; these exist to define common principles, roles, structures, and target capabilities for incident response.
- Strategic and tactical interoperable emergency communications planning has begun at the State and local levels (e.g., TICPs, SCIPs, FEMA, State and regional emergency communications planning).
- Common nomenclature initiatives for interoperability channels (e.g., NPSTC Channel Naming Report) are underway.
- FEMA has developed a DEC Integration Framework and continues to support both government and nongovernmental organizations in the development of plans and response frameworks and the identification of roles and responsibilities.
- FEMA's NIMS Integration Center is developing the National Emergency Responder Credentialing System (NERCS).
- Federal grant guidance (i.e., FY 2008 SAFECOM grant guidance; FY 2008 IECGP grant guidance) exists for migrating current radio practices to plain language standards.
- The Office for Interoperability and Compatibility (OIC), in coordination with OEC, is developing an SOP Development Guide, a Shared Channel Guide v2.0, and a brochure on plain language.
- DHS recently issued Federal Continuity Directive-1, which establishes continuity planning guidelines for Federal departments and agencies.
- The Office of Science and Technology Policy issued the National Communications System Directive (NCSD) 3-10, "Minimum Requirements for Continuity Communications Capabilities" as planning direction for communications capabilities that support continuity of operations.

Key Gaps and Obstacles Driving Action:
- There is inconsistent usage of plain language, interoperability channel naming conventions, interoperability frequencies, and SOPs.
- Nationwide adoption and usage of NIMS, NRF, and NERCS has been slow, because some users are often unfamiliar with the direction and intent of these policies.

- Inconsistent use of the Federal Communications Commission (FCC)-designated national interoperability channels has limited the effectiveness of this interoperability solution for emergency response communications systems operating in the same frequency band.

Supporting Initiatives and Milestones to Address Key Gaps:
- **Initiative 3.1: Standardize and implement common operational protocols and procedures.** A national adoption of plain-language radio practices and uniform common channel naming, along with the programming and use of existing national interoperability channels, will allow agencies across all disciplines to effectively share information on demand and in real time. Using common operational protocols and procedures avoids the confusion that the use of disparate coded language systems and various tactical interoperability frequencies can create. Use of the existing nationwide interoperability channels with common naming will immediately address interoperability requirements for agencies operating in the same frequency band.[25]

Recommended National Milestones:
- Within 6 months, OEC develops plain-language guidance in concert with State and local governments to address the unique needs of agencies/regions and disciplines across the Nation.
- Within 6 months, American National Standards Institute (ANSI) certifies, and emergency response accreditation organizations accept, the NPSTC Channel Naming Guide as the national standard for FCC-designated nationwide interoperability channels.
- Within 9 months, the National Integration Center's (NIC) Incident Management Systems Integration Division (IMSID) promotes plain-language standards and associated guidance.
- Within 12 months, grant policies for Federal programs that support emergency communications is coordinated, providing incentives for States to include plans to eliminate coded substitutions throughout the Incident Command System (ICS).
- Within 12 months, Federal agencies identify a uniform naming system for the National Telecommunications and Information Administration's (NTIA) designated nationwide interoperability channels, and this naming system is integrated into the NPSTC Guide.
- Within 18 months, DHS develops training and technical assistance programs for the National Interoperability Field Operations Guide (NIFOG);[26] programs an appropriate set of frequency-band-specific nationwide

---

[25] The National Telecommunications and Information Administration (NTIA) and members of the Interdepartment Radio Advisory Committee (IRAC), with support from the FCC, revised the NTIA Manual of Regulations and Procedures for Federal Radio Frequency Management. The NTIA amended the "Conditions for Use" and eliminated the requirement to establish an MOU between non-Federal and Federal entities on the use of the law enforcement (LE) and IR channels. The new conditions do, however, require the non-Federal entity to obtain a license and include a point of contact in the license application it submits to the FCC for use of the LE/IR channels.

[26] NIFOG is a collection of technical reference material to be used by radio technicians who are responsible for the radios to be used and applied during disaster response. NIFOG includes information from the National Interoperability Frequency Guide (NIFG), instructions on the use of NIFG, and other reference material. NIFOG is formatted to be a pocket-sized guide that is easy for radio technicians to carry.

interoperability channels into all existing emergency responder radios;[27] and preprograms an appropriate set of frequency-band-specific nationwide interoperability channels into emergency response radios that are manufactured or purchased through Federal funding as a standard requirement.
- o Within 24 months, all SCIPs reflect plans to eliminate coded substitutions throughout the ICS, and agencies incorporate the use of existing nationwide interoperability channels into SOPs, training, and exercises at the Federal, State, regional, local, and tribal levels.

- **Initiative 3.2: Implementation of the NIMS and the NRF across all levels of government.** Emergency response agencies across all levels of government should adopt and implement national-level policies and guidance to ensure a common approach to incident management and communications support. Implementation of these policies will establish clearly defined communications roles and responsibilities and enable integration of all communications elements as the ICS structure expands from the incident level to the national level.

Recommended National Milestones:
- o Within 12 months, all Federal, State, local, and tribal emergency response providers within UASI jurisdictions have implemented the Communications and Information Management section of the NIMS.

- **Initiative 3.3: Develop and implement model SOPs for specific events and all-hazards response.** SOPs comprise the range of informal and formal practices and procedures that guide emergency responder interactions and the use of interoperable emergency communications solutions. Agencies should develop, coordinate, and share best practices and procedures that encompass both operational and technical components. Command and control protocols should be NIMS-compliant and incorporate the ICS as an operational guide. Procedures for the activation, deployment, and deactivation of technical resources should be included, as well as roles and responsibilities for the operation, management, recovery, and continuity of equipment and infrastructure during an event. Agencies should identify procedures used to trigger and implement backup communications solutions should primary systems and solutions become unavailable. As the scale of an event expands, procedures for the integration of communications solutions become increasingly critical. Agencies must institute processes by which policies, practices, and procedures are regularly developed and reviewed for consistency across agencies.

Recommended National Milestones:

---

[27] Milestones in this area refer to the programming of an "appropriate set" of interoperability channels. This language is used in recognition that most radios used by emergency responders do not have the capacity to hold all of the national interoperability channels in addition to their required operational channels. Some radio channels are discipline-specific and are inappropriate to program in radios of other disciplines.

- o Within 6 months, DHS identifies and refine model SOPs for tactical communications and develops associated SOP training for emergency responders.
- o Within 12 months, DHS identifies and refine model SOPs for emergency communications during specific events and all-hazards response (beyond tactical communications).
- o Within 18 months, DHS collaborates with partner emergency communications organizations to disseminate model SOPs and will provide on a regional basis SOP training by mission type, event type, and all-hazards response to emergency response agencies.

Objective 4: Standards and Emerging Communication Technologies

Emerging technologies are integrated with current emergency communications capabilities through standards implementation, research and development, and testing and evalution.

The emergency response community recognizes that no single technological solution can address all emergency communications challenges or meet the needs of all agencies. The proprietary nature of many communications technologies creates an ongoing challenge to system connectivity and establishing interoperability among them. The presence of wireless data networks, Internet Protocol (IP)–based mobile communications devices, and location-based commercial services, however, are creating potential opportunities to enhance command and control and situational awareness. Accelerating the development of standards for existing and emerging technologies can address these technology challenges, and therefore improve communications during response operations for both routine and significant events.

Current Emergency Communications Activities:

- In cooperation with the emergency response community, the private sector, and the Federal Government, the Association pf Public-Safety Communications Officials (APCO), the National Association of State Technology Directors (NASTD), and the Telecommunications Industry Association (TIA) are developing a set of communications standards—the Project 25 (P25) suite of standards—for digital LMR.
- The standards for two of the eight P25 interfaces have been developed.
- OIC is establishing a P25 Compliance Assessment Program (CAP) to assess manufacturers' equipment for compliance with P25 standards.
- Major documents on Common Air Interface (CAI) standards have been completed and products that implement CAI standards are currently being fielded; other major P25 standards documents are being rapidly developed.
- Standards development for data exchange exists, to improve information-sharing capabilities among disparate emergency response software applications (e.g., Emergency Data Exchange Language [EDXL] standards including the Common Alerting Protocol, Distribution Element [DE], Hospital Availability Exchange [HAVE], Resource Messaging [RM], and the National Information Exchange Model [NIEM]).
- Broadband initiatives and standards development include the P25 Interface Committee's (APIC) Broadband Task Group (BBTG), Project MESA, and the NPSTC Broadband Working Group.
- Research and development (R&D) and testing and evaluation initiatives are driven by OIC (e.g., Voice over Internet Protocol [VoIP], Vocoder Testing, Multi-Band Radio, and Radio over Wireless Broadband [ROW-B]) and by the Department of Defense (DoD) (e.g., Joint Tactical Radio System [JTRS] and Joint Interoperability Test Command).
- The President's Spectrum Policy Initiative focuses on identifying methods that use emerging technologies, such as cognitive radio, to increase the efficiency and effectiveness of spectrum usage.

- Several States (e.g., Arizona, California, and Texas) are developing statewide "systems of systems" that leverage emerging technologies to establish interoperability among different levels of government and that span frequency bands.
- FEMA, following its DEC Integration Framework end-state architecture, is developing standardized deployable emergency communications capabilities that provide scalable and flexible voice, video, and data services.
- In the ongoing FCC rulemaking proceeding to establish a nationwide broadband emergency response network in the 700 Megahertz (MHz) band, OEC is coordinating with Federal emergency response agencies through the FPIC to ensure that such agencies have access to this broadband network and to ensure that Federal interests are represented in network-sharing negotiations with emergency response and commercial licensees.
- The U.S. Department of Justice (DOJ) CommTech program, with support from OIC, is funding R&D in the areas of cognitive and software-defined radio (SDR) and is providing input to the SDR forum to ensure emergency response needs are met by these technologies.
- DHS' Science and Technology Directorate's Command, Control, and Interoperability Division is leading a Common Operating Picture R&D program, and DOJ and other Federal entities are funding pilot projects to support State, local, and tribal emergency services activities.

Key Gaps and Obstacles Driving Action:
- Personnel responsible for designing or procuring communication systems are sometimes unaware of the status of communications standards.
- The number and diversity of emergency response agencies' procuring systems increases the complexity and difficulty of developing technologies to meet these user requirements.
- Standards development is hindered by the diverse requirements of independent emergency response organizations and agencies.
- Secure communications interoperability across Federal, State, local, and tribal emergency communications systems are often hindered by the Federal sector's use of encryption.
- There is insufficient information about the testing and assessment of emergency response technologies, which makes it difficult for emergency response agencies to make informed procurement decisions about technology for use both now and in the future.
- State and local government agencies do not consistently participate in standards-making bodies and development processes.
- A common view of existing incident conditions and resources is not readily available or easily shared across Federal, State, and local jurisdictions in a way that improves the understanding of the emergency or event

Supporting Initiatives and Milestones to Address Key Gaps:
- **Initiative 4.1: Adopt voluntary consensus standards for voice and data emergency response capabilities.** Voluntary consensus standards will enable agencies to make informed procurement decisions and to benefit from emerging

technologies. Compliance assessment programs provide a documented certification process for communications equipment and programs.

Recommended National Milestones:
- o Within 6 months, a P25 CAP is established to test equipment for compliance with approved interfaces.
- o Within 6 months, publish a specifications profile for VoIP and test using multiple manufacturers' equipment.
- o Within 12 months, DHS publishes the P25 CAP Summary Test Reports and manufacturers' Supplier's Declaration of Compliance (SDoC) for equipment.
- o Within 18 months, DHS makes standards and compliance information (e.g., the Authorized Equipment List [AEL] and the Standardized Equipment List [SEL]) available to educate and aid in communications equipment purchases.
- o Within 18 months, DHS establishes compliance strategies for non-land mobile radio emergency communications technologies.
- o Within 24 months, develop standards for the exchange of real-time situational information for emergency responders before, during, and after an incident.
- o Within 36 months, develop voluntary consensus standards for emergency communications data file structures and messaging formats.

- **Initiative 4.2: Research, develop, test, and evaluate new voice, video, and data solutions for emergency communications, based on user-driven needs and requirements.** New technologies, in conjunction with legacy systems, have the potential to eliminate current technological challenges such as a lack of available frequencies and the use of multiple frequency bands. Aggregating the demands of emergency response agencies during the development of requirements for these emerging technologies will increase the effectiveness of the private sector in developing standardized products and services.

Recommended National Milestones:
- o Within 3 months, DHS develops a process for emergency response agencies to collaborate with the private sector to aggregate user requirements.
- o Within 9 months, emergency response agencies identify and prioritize near-term (3–5 years) requirements.
- o Within 24 months, emergency response agencies develop, with the cooperation of private sector and other stakeholders, quality-of-service parameters for the most important near-term requirements.

- **Initiative 4.3: Transition to and/or integrate legacy systems with next-generation technologies based on voluntary consensus standards.**
Transitioning to next-generation technologies may provide emergency response agencies with easier-to-use and more functional capabilities, depending on their specific needs. The upcoming FCC narrowbanding deadline calls for non-Federal emergency response agencies operating in frequencies below 512 MHz to

transition from 25 kilohertz (kHz) to 12.5 kHz channels by 2013 to ensure spectrum efficiency. Federal grants can facilitate the migration and transition from legacy to approved open architecture and next-generation systems.

Recommended National Milestones:
   o Within 12 months, Federal grant policies are developed to encourage the migration to approved interoperable next generation systems.
   o Within 12 months, DHS publishes the results of pilots and evaluations of emerging technologies to emergency response agencies and private sector to support migration planning, standards development, and product development.
   o Within 12 months, DHS publishes information and materials that highlight system migration best practices, lessons learned, and the benefits of new system capabilities.

• **Initiative 4.4: Implement the Advanced Encryption Standard (AES) for Federal responders.** A standard nationwide encryption method will diminish the interoperability challenges faced by Federal responders (who previously used different methods) and will provide guidance to local and State agencies when working with Federal agencies.

Recommended National Milestones:
   o Within 18 months, achieve encrypted interoperability between Federal departments and agencies using the AES.
   o Within 18 months, publish a uniform standard for the AES for State, local, and tribal emergency responders who decide to use encryption.
   o Within 24 months, Federal grant policies are modified to facilitate the addition of an AES-encrypted feature for radio equipment used by State, local, and tribal emergency responders.

Objective 5: Emergency Responder Skills and Capabilities

Emergency responders have shared approaches to training and exercises, improved technical expertise, and enhanced response capabilties.

Training and exercises play a vital role in preparedness, readiness, and proficiency in accessing and using communications capabilities during emergency events. Preparedness is essential to ensuring that interoperable emergency communications equipment is well maintained, operational, and ready for deployment. Achieving appropriate levels of readiness and proficiency ensures that personnel can deploy, set up, and use equipment effectively, both on their own and in conjunction with other emergency responders. Conducting training and exercises helps emergency responders know their roles and be properly prepared to respond to a wide range of emergency events.

Current Emergency Communications Activities:
- Many State and local agencies have adopted NIMS training requirements, which are measured by Federal standards (e.g., NIMS 5-Year Training Plan).
- Incident Type III Communications Unit Leader (COML) training, which standardizes the emergency communications component of incident management, has been finalized. An awareness course that is intended to provide basic-level, communications-specific training to other command unit leaders, is under development.
- There are existing standards and guidelines for national preparedness exercises (e.g., the Homeland Security Exercise and Evaluation Program [HSEEP]) that help standardize and measure exercise efficiency.
- Large-scale preparedness exercises (e.g., Top Official [TOPOFF]) are being conducted with participants across levels of government, and some communications-specific exercises are being conducted (e.g., UASI TICP exercises) as well; additional annual exercises are generally conducted at the State and local levels.
- OEC is developing a planned events methodology to help emergency response officials design and execute interoperable communications plans for planned events.
- OEC is developing a Table Top Exercise Methodology to serve as a training aid in the reinforcement of interoperability practices and procedures for emergency responders.

Key Gaps and Obstacles Driving Action:
- Some emergency response agencies have not yet received NIMS training or have not adopted NIMS policies.
- A national standard for Type III COML training and certification has been developed, but has not yet been rolled out nationwide.
- A training curriculum for Communications Unit Technicians (COMT), Radio Operators (RADO), and other communications-unit positions has not yet been developed.
- Many emergency response agencies have available only a limited number of qualified technical staff to support daily operations and provide surge support for emergency communications.

- Private sector partners have not been consistently involved in training and exercises.
- There are insufficient communications-specific training courses and field exercises available to emergency responders, and there is a lack of coordination with the private sector on training and exercises.

Supporting Initiatives and Milestones to Address Key Gaps:
- **Initiative 5.1: Develop and implement national training programs and certification processes.** Standardized training programs should be established to deliver regular training to all emergency responders who use or manage communications resources. This training should be conducted within agencies to build knowledge and competency; across disciplines, jurisdictions, and levels of government; and with key private sector organizations as appropriate. Training programs should be comprehensive enough to address small-scale to large-scale events, to build the capability for coordinating with a full range of emergency response providers during all-hazards scenarios. Specific programs should include training for COMLs, COMTs, and the Federal Emergency Communications Coordinators (FECC). These programs should be evaluated regularly to determine their effectiveness and their impact on performance and proficiency levels, and to ensure the programs' existing content remains valid and that new content is incorporated as appropriate.

  Recommended National Milestones:
  - Within 12 months, DHS establishes national-level training programs and certification processes for COML, COMT, and FECC personnel.
  - Within 12 months, DHS finalizes and publishes ICS Communications Unit resource definitions (personnel and equipment).
  - Within 12 months, DHS develops a nationwide interoperability channel usage guide and ensures that shared channel training curriculum and courseware are available.
  - Within 18 months, DHS develops and uses standardize training and credentialing for COML and other ICS Communications Unit positions across the Nation.
  - Within 18 months, DHS establishes a certification process for other emergency communications users and providers, including COMT, dispatchers, and emergency response providers.

- **Initiative 5.2: Develop and inject standardized emergency communications performance objectives and evaluation criteria into operational exercises.** Incorporating standardized objectives and evaluation criteria into exercise programs will ensure the consistent evaluation of communications performance. By evaluating communications as part of operational exercises, leadership will acquire enhanced awareness and understanding of communications gaps. This understanding will ensure communications needs are prioritized appropriately.

  Recommended National Milestones:

o   Within 12 months, DHS establishes standardized exercise evaluation criteria based on the emergency communications performance objectives established in the DHS/FEMA Communications and Information Management Capability Framework.
o   Within 18 months, the exercise evaluation criteria are reviewed in preparation for release through technical working group meetings with stakeholders from the emergency response exercise community.
o   Within 24 months, the emergency communications criteria are incorporated into the Exercise Evaluation Guides of the DHS/FEMA HSEEP.

- **Initiative 5.3: Provide targeted training to improve skills and capabilities of technical staff.** Although most technicians receive formal communications training at the start of their careers as well as informal on-the-job training, ongoing or refresher training is not commonly provided because there are not enough qualified subject matter experts. Communications technicians typically are too burdened with daily operations and maintenance activities to engage in formal training campaigns. As a result, users who do not rely on communications equipment for their daily missions might be unfamiliar with the equipment and procedures for its use. Developing training programs for technical staff will increase the number and enhance the expertise of technical and operational resources.

Recommended National Milestones:
o   Within 12 months, DHS develops and disseminates training program guidance and curricula for emergency communications technical staff.
o   Within 18 months, DHS provides educational and training opportunities to emergency response agencies per requests through technical assistance programs.

Objective 6: System Life-Cycle Planning

All levels of government drive long-term advancements in emergency communications through integrated strategic planning procedures, appropriate resource allocations, and public-private partnerships.

Emergency response providers must upgrade and regularly maintain communications systems and capabilities to ensure effective operation; Federal grants can help meet these needs. However, initial capital investments in capabilities, enabled by grants, often are not accompanied by a plan for long-term sustainability. Grants should allow for expanded support of system upgrades, governance, planning, policies and procedures, and training and exercises. Federal agencies face a similar challenge in identifying sustainable funding mechanisms to upgrade and maintain communications systems. Public and private sector partners have their own core competencies and, thus, increased collaboration will add long-term value to emergency communications.

Current Emergency Communications Activities:
- OEC and OIC published an Interoperability Business Case to help emergency response officials develop a compelling business case for funding ongoing local interoperability efforts.[28]

Key Gaps and Obstacles Driving Action:
- Emergency communications are not viewed as a priority by many agencies; thus, resources are not allocated for participation in planning activities.
- Communications planning is not viewed as a priority by many agencies. DHS is working to ensure that limited Federal resources are targeted and expended more strategically on identified gaps, while maintaining adequate State and local flexibility.
- Many jurisdictions still pursue a short-term, technology-centric approach to solving emergency communications problems, but with a lack of comprehensive planning for the equally important governance mechanisms, SOPs, and regular training and exercises.
- Procurement decisions are often made without consulting neighboring jurisdictions or agencies.

Supporting Initiatives and Milestones to Address Key Gaps:
- **Initiative 6.1: Conduct system life-cycle planning to better forecast long-term funding requirements.** Providing planning and business case best practices through technical assistance will enable leadership to project the true cost of sustaining its communications system and allow budgeting for maintenance and eventual replacement. Grant funding investment justifications from States and spending within the Federal Government should be prioritized to support cooperative, regional (intrastate and interstate) system planning efforts.

---

[28] The Interoperability Business Case is available on the SAFECOME website at:
http://www.safecomprogram.gov/SAFECOM/library/grant/1336_interoperabilitybusiness.htm

Recommended National Milestones:
- o Within 12 months, DHS will revise current guidance documents that specify best practices for achieving basic operable communications while planning for interoperability.
- o Within 18 months, DHS will collect and share best practices to assist emergency response agencies in identifying emergency communications system life-cycle benchmarks to enhance long-term cost planning and budgeting.
- o Within 24 months, Federal grant programs require system life-cycle plans for all communications systems purchased with Federal grant dollars.

- **Initiative 6.2: Expand the use of public and private sector partnerships related to emergency communications.** Although the private sector owns more than 85 percent of critical infrastructure, government and emergency response agencies own and operate communications systems that support their critical missions, including defense, law enforcement, and emergency response.[29] The private sector's capabilities include fixed, mobile, and rapidly deployable networks, assets, and facilities that can help ensure the success of emergency communications. A more formal understanding of the specific service offerings and capabilities of private sector organizations is required to better leverage existing and future communications capabilities.

Recommended National Milestones:
- o Within 12 months, DHS convenes a summit of emergency responders and private sector representatives to identify and make recommendations on additional public-private sector partnerships to improve emergency communications.

- **Initiative 6.3: Assess existing Federal mission-critical wireless capabilities and upgrade and modernize them according to mission needs.** In many areas, Federal departments and agencies are still working to achieve the basic operability to achieve their missions. Federal agencies require high-quality, secure, and reliable communications systems to support their mission-critical operations. Whether facing a natural disaster or other emergency event, tactical communications is a tool that enables Federal emergency responders to perform their jobs, ultimately protecting against the loss of life and property. Federal agencies must develop and implement strategies to meet modernization mandates and upgrade infrastructure to attain resilient communications systems.

Recommended National Milestones:
- o Within 6 months, all Federal departments and agencies assess existing communications capabilities and compare them with the capabilities needed to complete their missions.

---

[29] *The National Infrastructure Protection Plan*: Communications Sector-Specific Plan, p. 11.

- Within 12 months, all Federal agencies determine priorities, plan budgets and schedules, and design required upgrades to mission-critical subscriber and infrastructure equipment.

- **Initiative 6.4: Enhance emergency communications system survivability using redundant and resilient system designs.** Disaster events can adversely affect the performance of the communications systems that agencies use for emergency response. Emergency response agencies must identify the events that can disrupt the communications system components (e.g., radio repeaters, backhaul circuits, and power systems) and develop plans to enhance survivability. Implementing redundant infrastructure, developing resilience strategies, identifying recovery time objectives, and exercising communications continuity plans will improve communications system survivability.

  Recommended National Milestones:
  - Within 12 months, DHS will coordinate with RECCWGs to conduct impact analyses of communications systems to identify the impact from the affects of the disaster and disruption scenarios analyzed.
  - Within 18 months, DHS will coordinate with RECCWGs to ensure that all Federal, State, local, and tribal emergency response providers have developed and implemented communications continuity plans for maintaining or recovering and stabilizing operations during and following disaster events.
  - Within 24 months, DHS will coordinate with RECCWGs to ensure that all Federal, State, local, and tribal emergency response providers have coordinated communications continuity exercises and established crisis communications procedures and policies.

Objective 7: Disaster Communications Capabilities

The Nation has integrated preparedness, mitigation, and response and recovery capabilities to communicate during significant events.

Significant events require maximum emergency response coordination. Adding to the complexity of a response during events is the loss of communications infrastructure and capabilities resulting from destruction caused by all hazards. To adequately react to the potential loss or lack of capacity of communications capabilities, agencies must proactively develop contingency and continuity plans, pre-plan the placement and delivery of deployable communications assets and resources, and participate in training and exercise programs that include disaster communications-response scenarios. Appendix 3 provides an overview of primary emergency response agencies and their programs, systems, and services.

Current Emergency Communications Activities:
- The Mobile Emergency Response Support (MERS) component of the FEMA DEC describes DHS' primary rapid and deployable emergency communications capability in support of Federal, State, and local responders for the first 96 hours following an incident.
- The FEMA DEC has been working with individual States and Territories since 2006 to identify potential communications gaps during responses and to mitigate the gaps by pre-planning response packages tailored for each State. FEMA plans to complete 23 State and Territory DEC Annexes by 2008.
- The Joint Network Nodes (JNN) is the bridge between the Warfighter Information Network–Tactical (WIN-T), a high-capacity network system that enables units and command centers to communicate while on the move, and the Army's 30-year-old legacy voice communications system, Mobile Subscriber Equipment.
- The National Guard Bureau (NGB) has deployed the Joint Incident Site Communications Capability (JISCC) in 56 States and Territories, a transit case-based system that includes satellite reach-back communications, incident site communications, interoperability gateway communications, and command post integration and support equipment.
- The PSIC Grant Program funded $75 million in Strategic Technology Reserves (STR) for States and Territories. Investments were made in deployable assets, radio caches, infrastructure enhancements, and satellite technology.
- Some State, local, and tribal agencies are developing statewide communications systems and shared systems to expand capabilities.
- Emergency response providers are enhancing communications continuity of operations plans (e.g., backup and mobile/deployable solutions, and strategic technology reserves).
- Federal priority communications and reporting services are available for priority access and telecommunication system restoration and recovery (e.g., Government Emergency Telecommunications Service [GETS], Telecommunications Service Priority [TSP], Wireless Priority Service [WPS], and Disaster Information Reporting System [DIRS]).
- The U.S. Northern Command (USNORTHCOM), established in 2002, provides Defense Support of Civil Authorities (DSCA) for domestic emergencies, both

natural and man-made, and provides command and control of DoD personnel and DoD agency and component resources.[30]

Key Gaps and Obstacles Driving Action:
- The emergency response community needs more education about Federal agencies' strategic, policy, and operational capabilities for emergency communications.
- There is no integration framework that describes disaster communications services, the community of agencies and companies that provide these services, and the procedures for integrating these services and communities.
- Communications planning activities related to disaster events that may overwhelm or destroy communications systems are limited.
- There are multiple deployable and disaster communications asset data sets, but there is no comprehensive and accurate data set that could be used to integrate communications during a disaster.
- There is a need for disaster emergency communications technical standards to ensure uniform interoperability in terms of design specifications, methods of systems employment, processes, and/or operating practices. Some standards are mandatory and some are voluntary.
- Many agencies have a limited ability to identify replacement equipment and operations and maintenance funding to ensure the basic operability of their primary tactical systems.
- The ability to communicate across agencies and jurisdictions is limited by the fragmented nature of spectrum and by the requirement to operate on noncontiguous bands.
- There is no standardized means for identifying individuals, both emergency response agencies and commercial communications providers, authorized to access and receive information about the disaster area.
- Few agencies conduct communications infrastructure threat and vulnerability assessments as part of emergency communications planning on critical communications assets.
- Many emergency response agencies are unaware of the priority services available from the Federal Government during emergencies.
- Many States do not have MOUs or frequency agreements with NGB to guide the use of the JISCC system.

Priority Initiatives and Milestones to Address Key Gaps:
- **Initiative 7.1: Provide an integration framework for disaster communications operations and response to ensure that the Federal Government can effectively fulfill requests during incident response.** Although disaster communications capabilities are owned by many agencies and private sector entities, there is currently a limited understanding of how these capabilities would be integrated during operations. Following Hurricane Katrina, deployable assets were in use across the operations areas, but there was limited coordination. In addition, a common operating picture was not available to senior leaders across government.

---

[30] Government Accountability Office (GAO), Report to Congressional Requesters: Homeland Defense, April 2008.

Recommended National Milestones:
- o Within 6 months, DHS develops Disaster Tactical Communications Requirements Analysis to assess Federal, State, and local disaster emergency communications functional support areas (e.g., restoration, mission operations/team support, facility, tactical, and planning and coordination).
- o Within 12 months, based on the Disaster Tactical Communications Requirements Analysis, DHS develops an Integration Framework and Concept of Operations (CONOPS) describing how disaster communications requirements are filled and integrated at the national, regional, and incident levels.
- o Within 24 months, DHS establish the capability to track and monitor Federal assets during a response scenario.

- **Initiative 7.2: Implement disaster communications planning and preparedness activities.** Identifying critical communications vulnerabilities and developing mitigation strategies is important for all agencies with operational responsibilities during major events. Agencies should evaluate the readiness posture of communications centers (e.g., Public Safety Answering Points [PSAP]) and emergency response and commercial networks that may be vulnerable to weather damage, flooding, and man-made disasters. The vulnerabilities identified should be a primary focus of disaster planning and preparedness activities. System planning activities should account for the availability of alternative and backup communications solutions and redundant pathways (i.e., provided by different vendors) to support communications if primary capabilities become unavailable.

Recommended National Milestones:
- o Within 12 months, RECCWGs will work with State and local agencies to assess priority State vulnerabilities that, without mitigation, could hamper command and control of and delivery of critical mission operations.
- o Within 12 months, DHS develops and publishes best practices and methodologies that promote the incorporation of vulnerability assessments as part of emergency communications planning.
- o Within 24 months, develop plans and procedures to enhance emergency 911 systems and PSAP communications.
- o Within 24 months, complete disaster communications training and exercises for all 56 States and Territories.
- o Within 24 months, all Federal, State, local, and tribal agencies in UASIs have defined alternate/backup capabilities in emergency communications plans.

- **Initiative 7.3: Leverage existing and emerging technologies to expand and integrate disaster communications capabilities among emergency response providers.** Deployable communications technologies can provide robust voice, video, and data capabilities for agencies requiring communications during disasters.

Packaging these capabilities to be quickly deployable and easily integrated and interoperable is a significant challenge. DHS will work across the government and the private sector to enable more effective pre-positioning and integration of existing and cutting-edge technologies.

Recommended National Milestones:
- o Within 12 months, using the results of the Disaster Tactical Communications Requirements Analysis, DHS identifies a list of technologies that meet the majority of requirements identified.
- o Within 18 months, DHS provides a Disaster Communications Capability List to be included in the AEL and the SEL that provides an overview of approved interoperable or standardized equipment that should be used during response.
- o Within 24 months, DHS will reassess its pre-positioning framework to evaluate whether it best meets national disaster communications needs.

- **Initiative 7.4: Accelerate the implementation of emergency communications components in the NRF, specifically, national access and credentialing.** NRF establishes a comprehensive, national, all-hazards approach to domestic incident response and is used broadly in an operational context for incident management activities related to pre-incident prevention and post-incident response and recovery. The Joint Field Office (JFO) DEC Branch coordinates Federal communications support to response efforts during incidents requiring a Federal response. The JFO DEC Branch also coordinates communications support to Federal, State, local, and tribal governments and emergency responders when their systems have been impacted and provides communications and information technology support to the JFO and its field teams. Comprehensive use of NRF will ensure consistent operations across the Nation and will reduce the risk of miscommunication among emergency response agencies. In addition to ensuring common use of NRF, ensuring suitable credentialing for all responders who require access to an incident site is critical to rapid and effective response and recovery. Depending on the size and scope of the incident, those who require access and credentials may include Federal, State, local, and tribal emergency responders, as well as NGO and private sector telecommunications infrastructure provider response personnel.

Recommended National Milestones:
- o Within 24 months, DHS develops a national access and credentialing guidelines that provides emergency responders, including critical commercial communications providers, with a means of identifying individuals eligible to access and receive information about the disaster area.

- **Initiative 7.5: Implement systems and procedures that ensure the Federal Government's ability to establish situational awareness, develop a common operating picture, and provide timely and consistent information during crises.** The collection and dissemination of information in preparation for and during an event is essential to mitigate threats and to respond efficiently. Situational awareness includes predicting the occurrence of a natural disaster or an attack; knowing the extent of damage that results from an event; having an operating picture that includes the status of response activities, critical infrastructures, and public health; and understanding plans for response and restoration. Situational awareness processes and activities serve to improve and reduce barriers to information sharing.

Recommended National Milestones:
- o Within 12 months, DHS establishes a plan for an integrated asset tracking system to enable information sharing across the national, regional, and incident levels.

- **Initiative 7.6: Promote the use of and expand the capabilities of priority services programs (e.g., GETS, WPS, and TSP) to next-generation networks.** Priority access services are critical to the ability of emergency responders to access telecommunications resources during an event. Major events result in high-level use of telecommunications resources by emergency responders and the public. It is critical that emergency response providers have access to telecommunications resources when needed to enable information exchange. Currently, the National Communications System sponsors several priority access services (i.e., GETS, TSP, and WPS) that are available for use by Federal, State, local, and tribal agencies. Based on mission requirements, agencies across levels of government should leverage these services to ensure access to telecommunications resources when needed. In addition, planning is needed to ensure the availability of these services as networks transition to next-generation technologies.

Recommended National Milestones:
- o Within 18 months, OEC will work with statewide coordinators to promote the availability and use of priority access services throughout their States or Territories.
- o Within 24 months, DHS establishes plans to transition priority access services to next-generation networks.

IV. Implementing and Measuring NECP Achievement

The success of the NECP requires the commitment of all emergency response disciplines at all levels of government. Achieving its goals and priority objectives will require coordination across geographical, political, and cultural jurisdictions and boundaries. Therefore, this Plan provides strategic direction and guidance that Congress, Federal departments and agencies, State, local, and tribal government officials, and the private sector can use to identify future actions to address communications deficiencies.

4.1 Implementation

OEC, within the National Protection and Programs Directorate (NPPD) of DHS, is designated the primary Federal agent charged with overseeing NECP implementation. In this role, OEC will monitor achievement of the NECP's recommended milestones and initiatives and will coordinate with its stakeholders to assess progress in reaching this Plan's goals. OEC's current levers and incentives for driving NECP implementation include the provision of technical assistance to State, regional, local, and tribal government officials; grant policies and coordination of DHS-administered grant programs (e.g., IECGP); and coordination of Federal activities through the ECPC and FPIC. In addition, OEC will use statutory reporting requirements to monitor and report on progress towards implementing the NECP (e.g., State annual reports under the IECGP, RECCWG annual reports, ECPC annual strategic assessment, and OEC's assessment and biennial progress reports).

Within the first year of the NECP implementation, OEC will partner with key stakeholders to determine appropriate metrics for the objectives and initiatives. OEC will provide a status report in its Biennial Progress Report to Congress, due February 2010. Implementation of the NECP will be a coordinated effort among all levels of government including those listed below.

Executive and Legislative Branches—The NECP will provide the legislative and executive branches with recommended initiatives and national milestones that will inform them of emergency communications priorities, activities, and resource allocations for consideration and action.

Federal Agencies—For the first time, the NECP documents the challenges of coordinating emergency communications efforts at the Federal level. Federal responders also must have the capability to work with State and local responders in a time of emergency. Two key Federal partnerships will be used to implement the NECP. Through the ECPC, Federal implementation of the NECP will be a collaborative effort, allowing all stakeholders to have a better understanding of the achievements at this level. Through FPIC, Federal response organizations will work with State and local agencies and governments to improve communications and resource sharing.

State, Local, and Tribal Governments—The NECP provides guidance for improved emergency communications to State, local, and tribal agencies and governments to better focus Federal funding dollars and provides a forum for regional planning and participation. State, local, and tribal governments should strive to align with the NECP and implement key initiatives.

Private Sector—The NECP identifies private sector support to communications during emergencies and recovery efforts and provides consistent direction for private sector involvement in standards development, advanced communications technologies, and services development and deployment.

4.2 Metrics

DHS will use future versions of the following reports and assessments to help assess progress toward achieving the goals of the NECP:
- ECPC Annual Strategic Assessment
- RECCWG Annual Report
- OEC's Biennial Progress Report
- OEC's National Communications Capabilities Report.

DHS, through OEC and the FEMA RECCWGs, will collaborate with State homeland security advisors and statewide interoperability coordinators to develop appropriate methodologies for measuring progress toward these goals.

4.3 Future Requirements

As reflected in Initiatives 1.2 and 5.2, DHS will collaborate with Federal, State, regional, and local governments and the private sector to develop a more comprehensive and targeted set of evaluation criteria for defining, measuring, and assessing communications requirements across the Nation. To prevent duplicative reporting requirements for stakeholders, assessment efforts will leverage existing reporting requirements (e.g., SCIPs, TICP, and State preparedness reports) and grant program applications (e.g., IECGP and HSGP). Evaluation criteria will be consistent with DHS implementation of the National Preparedness Guidelines and the TCL.

V. Conclusion

Ultimately, the NECP's goals cannot be achieved without the support, dedication, and commitment of the stakeholders who have been involved in developing this Plan. The Federal, State, local, tribal, and private sectors must work together and support each other to achieve nationwide operability, interoperability, and continuity of emergency communications. The NECP provides stakeholders with a shared strategy to mitigate the unique challenges that effective communication presents. By taking the NECP to action, this diverse community can truly achieve a unified vision that allows emergency responders to communicate as needed, on demand, and as authorized, at all levels of government and across all disciplines.

NECP Appendices

Appendix 1:   NECP Legislative Requirements Compliance Matrix

Appendix 2:   Alignment with National Strategies, Planning Initiatives, and Key Authorities

Appendix 3:   Key Federal Emergency Communications Initiatives, Programs, Systems, and Services

Appendix 4:   DHS Organizations with Responsibilities and Programs Supporting Emergency Communications

Appendix 5:   The SAFECOM Interoperability Continuum

Appendix 6:   NECP Stakeholder Coordination

Appendix 7:   NECP Source Documents

Appendix 8:   Glossary of Terms

Appendix 9:   Acronyms

Appendix 1:   NECP Legislative Requirements Compliance Matrix

Exhibit A1-1 is a matrix that maps the National Emergency Communications Plan (NECP) to the Title XVIII legislative requirements.

Exhibit A1-1: Matrix of Title XVIII Legislative Requirements with NECP Sections

No.	Title XVIII Legislative Requirements	NECP Section(s)
1	Include recommendations developed in consultation with the Federal Communications Commission (FCC) and the National Institute of Standards and Technology (NIST) for a process for *expediting national voluntary consensus standards* for interoperable emergency communications equipment	Section 3 – Objective 4: Standards & Emerging Technologies
2	Identify the appropriate *capabilities* necessary for emergency response providers and relevant government officials to *continue to communicate* in the event of natural disasters, acts of terrorism, and other man-made disasters	Section 2.3 – Capabilities Needed
3	Identify the *appropriate interoperable emergency communications capabilities* necessary for Federal, State, local, and tribal governments in the event of natural disasters, acts of terrorism, and other man-made disasters	Section 2.3 – Capabilities Needed
4	Recommend both *short-term and long-term solutions* for ensuring that emergency response providers and relevant government officials can *continue to communicate* in the event of natural disasters, acts of terrorism, and other man-made disasters	Section 3 – Initiatives and Milestones for Objectives 2, 3, 5, 7
5	Recommend both *short-term and long-term solutions* for deploying interoperable emergency communications systems for Federal, State, local, and tribal governments throughout the Nation, including through the provision of *existing and emerging technologies*	Section 3 – Initiatives and Milestones for Objectives 3, 4, 5, 6
6	Identify how *Federal departments and agencies* that respond to natural disasters, acts of terrorism, and other man-made disasters *can work effectively with State, local, and tribal governments* in all States, and with other entities	Section 3 – Objectives 1, 2, 7
7	Identify *obstacles to deploying interoperable* emergency communications capabilities nationwide and *recommend short-term and long-term measures* to overcome those obstacles, including recommendations for *multi-jurisdictional coordination* among Federal, State, local, and tribal governments	Section 3 – For all objectives, see "Key Gaps Driving Action" for obstacles and relevant "Initiatives" for recommendations
8	Recommend *goals and time frames* for the deployment of emergency, *command-level communications systems* and develop a timetable for the deployment of interoperable emergency communications systems nationwide	• Section 2.2 – Goals • Section 3 – Relevant Initiatives and Milestones for all Objectives
9	Recommend appropriate measures that emergency response providers should employ to ensure *continued operation of relevant governmental communications infrastructure*	Section 3 – Initiatives 4.2, 4.3, 6.2, 6.4, 7.2, 7.3
10[31]	(HR 1) Set a *date, including interim benchmarks*, by which State, local, and tribal governments, and Federal agencies expect to achieve a *baseline level of national interoperable communications*	Section 2.2 – Goals

---

[31] This NECP requirement was added by H.R. 1, *Implementing Recommendations of the 9/11 Commission Act of 2007* (Public Law 110-53), which was signed into law August 3, 2007.

Appendix 2: Alignment with National Strategies, Planning Initiatives, and Key Authorities

The NECP has been designed to complement and support overarching homeland security and emergency communications legislation, strategies, and initiatives. The NECP applies guidance from these authorities, including key principles and priorities, to establish the first national strategic plan focused exclusively on improving emergency communications for emergency response providers nationwide. Moreover, the NECP provides a critical link between national communications priorities and strategic and tactical planning at the regional, State, and local levels. Exhibit A2-1 illustrates the linkage between the NECP and primary emergency communications authorities.

Exhibit A2-1: Key Homeland Security and Emergency Communications Authorities

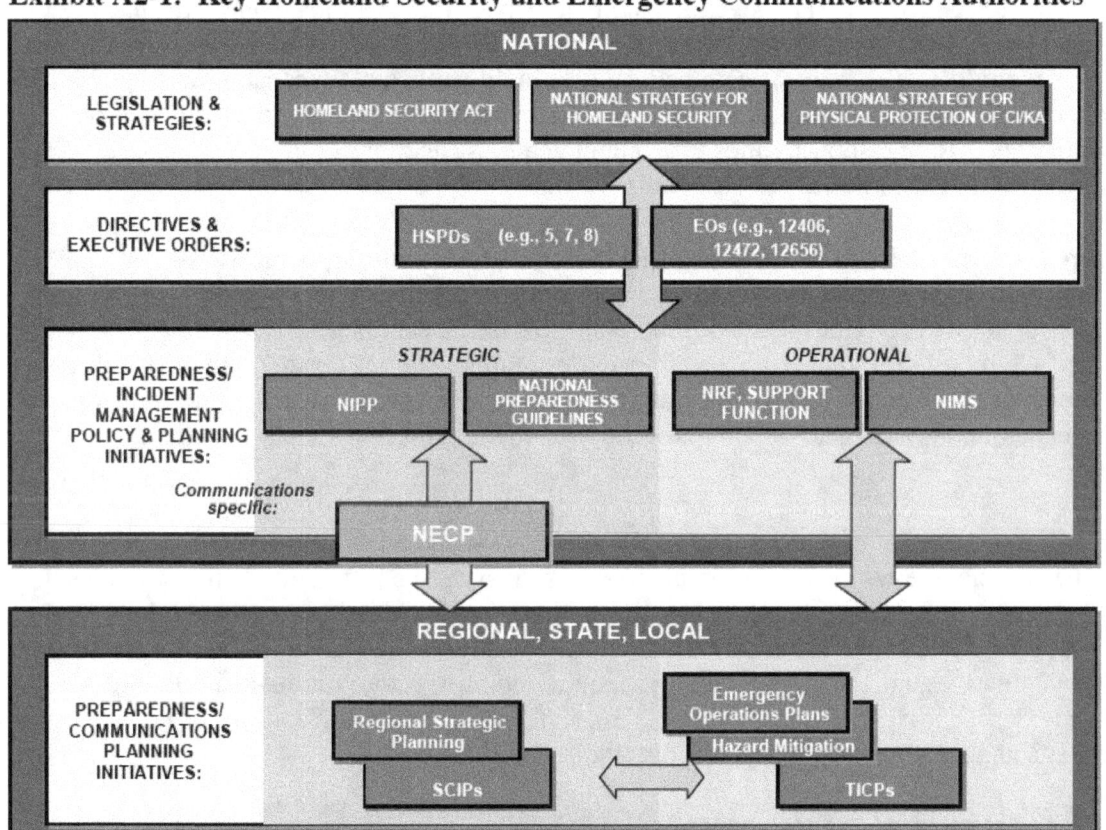

Various emergency communications authorities shape, and are reflected in, the NECP—

- **Legislation**—The *Homeland Security Act of 2002*, as amended by the *Homeland Security Appropriations Act of 2007*, provides the primary authority for the homeland security mission and establishes a foundation for emergency communications efforts nationwide. Other legislation identifies priorities at the national level and establishes departmental responsibilities and processes related to national preparedness and emergency communications.

- **Strategies**—National strategies provide the vision and strategic direction for emergency communications elements of the homeland security mission. For example, the *National Strategy for Homeland Security* emphasizes situational awareness as an incident management principle and stresses the importance of communications interoperability and survivability. This strategy and others, such as the *National Strategy for the Physical Protection of Critical Infrastructure and Key Assets*, identify high-level actions and priorities for national preparedness related to communications (e.g., improving public safety communications, supporting development of interoperable, secure communications systems, coordinating interoperability standards, developing redundant communications networks, and promoting common standards and terminology for equipment and training).

- **Federal Directives and Executive Orders**—These documents set national policies and executive mandates for specific initiatives, programs, and associated responsibilities. For example, *Homeland Security Presidential Directive 5 (HSPD 5)* required the Department of Homeland Security (DHS) to develop and implement a *National Incident Management System (NIMS)* and the *National Response Plan (NRP)*. *HSPD 8* mandated the development of a *National Preparedness Goal* to help entities build and maintain capabilities to prevent, protect, respond, and recover from major incidents. Other directives and executive orders identify and assign responsibilities for communications functions (e.g., spectrum, critical infrastructure, telecommunications continuity, and alert and warning).

- **Preparedness/ Incident Management DHS Policy and Planning Initiatives**—National policy and planning initiatives follow from legislation, directives, and orders, implementing the programs and activities described therein. Consistent with these DHS policy initiatives, the NECP focuses on improving the emergency communications posture nationwide through strategic goals, objectives, initiatives, and milestones. Following are descriptions of some key Federal policy and planning initiatives for incident management and emergency response:

  - **National Infrastructure Protection Plan (NIPP)**—The NIPP, and supporting sector-specific plans, establishes a comprehensive risk management framework that provides the unifying structure for integrating existing and future critical infrastructure and key resource (CI/KR) protection efforts into a single national program. The NIPP specifies key initiatives, milestones, and metrics required to protect the Nation's CI/KR and provides a coordinated approach that defines the roles and responsibilities of Federal, State, and local governments as well as the private sector.

  - **National Incident Management System (NIMS)**—Provides a nationwide template for incident management, establishing uniform doctrine for command and management, resources, communications, information management, and supporting technologies. Specific to communications, NIMS defines concepts and principles (e.g., interoperability, reliability, resiliency), management characteristics (e.g., communications types, planning, equipment standards, training), and standards and formats (e.g., radio usage procedures, plain language), which are clearly reflected in the NECP.

  - **National Response Framework (NRF)**—Establishes a comprehensive, national, all-hazards approach to domestic incident response. The NRF is used broadly in an operational context for incident management activities related to pre-incident prevention and post-incident response and recovery.

A – 4

– **National Preparedness Guidelines**—Provides readiness targets, priorities, standards for assessments and strategies, and a system for assessing the Nation's overall level of preparedness. The guidelines consist of standard planning tools, such as the Target Capabilities List (TCL), that agencies should develop and maintain to provide guidance on the specific capabilities and levels of capability related to the homeland security mission. In the area of communications, the TCL stresses the importance of operable, interoperable, and redundant communications during an emergency, and provides measures and metrics to define how quickly and how effectively critical communications tasks should be performed. The NECP was developed consistent with TCL guidelines and preparedness objectives, and should help local communities meet their requirements under TCL.

- **State, Regional, and Local Planning**—The NECP provides a critical link between national priorities and strategic and tactical planning at the regional, State, and local levels. DHS has analyzed the progress and gaps identified through State and local planning efforts in developing the NECP's priorities, initiatives, and associated actions. In turn, these national priorities will be incorporated into existing and future regional, State, and local planning efforts.

Descriptions of the key legislation, strategies, directives and executive orders, and policy initiatives that shape the emergency communications policy environment are provided below.

A2.1 Legislation

Exhibit A2-2 describes the key legislation that guides national efforts to ensure communications during crises.

Exhibit A2-2: Key Legislation

Name	Date	Description
The Communications Act of 1934, *amended by the Telecommunications Act of 1996*	June 19, 1934; February 8, 1996	Authorizes the Executive Branch to manage communications during wartime and non-wartime emergencies, and creates the Federal Communications Commission (FCC) as the chief regulatory authority for communications technologies. The FCC works to enhance emergency communications capabilities and addresses critical spectrum issues within the Public Safety and Homeland Security Bureau and in coordination with the National Telecommunications and Information Administration (NTIA).
Defense Production Act of 1950	September 8, 1950	Ensures timely availability of the products, materials, and services needed to meet national defense and emergency preparedness requirements, and provides an operating structure to support a timely, comprehensive response by industry in a national emergency situation.
Information Technology Management Reform Act of 1996 (P.L. 104-106)	February 10, 1996	Specifies that the National Institute of Standards and Technology (NIST) develop standards, guidelines, and associated methods and techniques for Federal computer systems. Federal Information Processing Standards (FIPS) are developed by NIST when there are no existing voluntary standards to address the Federal requirements for the interoperability of different systems, portability of data and software, and computer security.
The Balanced Budget Act of 1997; Deficit Reduction Act (P.L. 109-171)	August 5, 1997; February 8, 2006	Requires the FCC to allocate 24 MHz of spectrum in the 700 MHz band to public safety. The Deficit Reduction Act sets a firm deadline of February 2009 by which television broadcasters must vacate the occupied spectrum for the public safety community.
10 U.S.C. Section 372-380, *Military Support for Civilian Law Enforcement Agencies, as amended*	1998	Establishes protocols for the development, use, support, and maintenance of communications equipment shared by the U.S. military and local law enforcement agencies.

Name	Date	Description
The Robert T. Stafford Disaster Relief and Emergency Assistance Act	November 23, 1988	Establishes processes by which the Federal government can provide assistance to State, local, and tribal governments, individuals, and nongovernmental organizations (NGO) for all-hazards emergency response and recovery. This includes establishment and use of temporary communications systems in anticipation of or during an emergency.
Disaster Mitigation Act of 2000 (P.L. 106-390)	October 30, 2000	Amends the Stafford Act and requires State mitigation plans as a condition of disaster assistance.
The Homeland Security Act of 2002 (Public Law [P.L.] 107-296)	November 25, 2002	Establishes the DHS as an executive department of the United States and specifies significant responsibilities associated with emergency preparedness, response, and recovery, including emergency communications and critical infrastructure. Includes provisions for coordinating or (as appropriate) consolidating communications systems related to homeland security at all levels of government.
Federal Information Security Management Act of 2002 (part of P.L. 107-347)	December 17, 2002	Requires Federal agencies to develop a comprehensive information technology security program to ensure the effectiveness of information security controls over information resources that support Federal operations and assets.
The Intelligence Reform and Terrorism Prevention Act (P.L. 108-458)	December 17, 2004	Addresses national preparedness by identifying the need for a nationwide incident command system; establishes the Office for Interoperability and Compatibility (OIC) for the enhancement of public safety interoperability; and calls for studies on interoperable communications standards, spectrum, and strategies to meet public safety communications requirements.
The Homeland Security Appropriations Act of 2007 (P.L. 109-295), *including the 21st Century Emergency Communications Act of 2006*	October 4, 2006	Includes Title VI, the Post-Katrina Emergency Management Reform Act, which reorganizes the Federal Emergency Management Agency (FEMA), amends the Stafford Act, and addresses emergency communications. In addition, the legislation amends the Homeland Security Act of 2002 to add Title XVIII–Emergency Communications, establishing the Office of Emergency Communications (OEC) and specifying its responsibilities. Transfers existing programs (e.g., Integrated Wireless Network, Interoperable Communications Technical Assistance Program) and elements of other programs (e.g., SAFECOM) to OEC and assigns new responsibilities (e.g., National Emergency Communications Plan, National Baseline Assessment, and outreach and coordination).
Implementing the Recommendations of the 9/11 Commission Act of 2007 (P.L. 110-53)	August 3, 2007	Amends the Homeland Security Act of 2002 to establish the Urban Area Security Initiative to provide grants to assist high-risk metropolitan areas to prevent, prepare for, protect against, and respond to terrorist acts. Establishes the State Homeland Security Grant Program to assist State, local, and tribal governments to prevent, prepare for, protect against, and respond to terrorist acts. Directs the Secretary to establish the Interoperable Emergency Communications Grant Program to make grants to States to carry out initiatives to improve international, national, regional, statewide, local, and tribal, interoperable emergency communications.

A2.2 Strategy

Exhibit A2-3 describes the key homeland security strategies that provide direction for emergency communications elements of the homeland security mission.

Exhibit A2-3: Key Homeland Security Strategies

Name	Date	Description
National Strategy for the Physical Protection of Critical Infrastructures and Key Assets	February 2003	Identifies the policy, goals, objectives, and principles for actions needed to *secure the infrastructures and assets vital to national security, governance, public health and safety, economy, and public confidence.* Directs DHS to partner with the private sector to understand the risks associated with the physical vulnerabilities of critical infrastructures and key assets.
National Strategy to Secure Cyberspace	February 2003	Establishes priorities and initiatives to improve the physical security of cyber systems and communications, including interdependencies.
National Strategy for Homeland Security	October 2007 (revised)	Provides a common framework to guide the Nation's homeland security efforts toward achieving four primary goals: (1) prevent and disrupt terrorist attacks; (2) protect people, critical infrastructures, and key resources; (3) respond and recover from incidents; and (4) strengthen the homeland security foundation for long-term success. Specific to communications, the strategy emphasizes situational awareness as a critical incident management principle and stresses the importance of communications interoperability and survivability.

A2.3 Directives and Executive Orders

Exhibit A2-4 describes the key directives and executive orders for ensuring communications during crises.

Exhibit A2-4: Key Directives and Executive Orders

Name	Date	Description
Executive Order 12046, *Relating to the Transfer of Telecommunications Functions*	March 27, 1978	Delegates presidential responsibilities for management of the Federal electromagnetic spectrum to the Secretary of Commerce. Provides for the continuation of the Inter-department Radio Advisory Committee (IRAC) to assist the Secretary in exercising the delegated presidential authority.
Department of Commerce Organization Order 10-10	May 9, 1978	Establishes the National Telecommunications and Information Administration (NTIA), delegates presidential responsibilities for management of the electromagnetic spectrum to its administrator, and establishes the administrator's authority and responsibility for all radio communications systems operated by the Federal government.
Presidential Directive 53, *National Security Telecommunications Policy*	November 15, 1979	Reaffirms the need for connectivity for the Nation's leaders and the ability to respond, restore, and recover the national telecommunication infrastructure in all emergencies.
Executive Order 12372, *Intergovernmental Review of Federal Programs*	July 14, 1982	Intends to foster intergovernmental partnerships by providing opportunities for State, regional, and local coordination and review of proposed Federal financial assistance.
National Security Decision Directive 97, *National Security Telecommunications Policy*	June 13, 1983	Sets requirements for emergency restoration and recovery of communications that support the Nation's leaders, worldwide intelligence, and diplomacy. Confirms the provision of interoperable, reliable, and secure communications for the President and his chief advisors as a national priority.
Executive Order 12472, *Assignment of National Security and Emergency Preparedness (NS/EP) Telecommunications Functions*	April 3, 1984	Establishes the National Communications System (NCS) as the Federal interagency system to ensure that the national telecommunications infrastructure is responsive to the NS/EP needs of national leaders, the military, the Intelligence Community, and emergency responders. Establishes NCS as the focal point for joint industry/government NS/EP communications planning and directs the establishment of a national coordinating center. Establishes DHS as the agency responsible for planning, providing, operating, and maintaining telecommunications services and facilities as part of the National Emergency Management Systems. Identifies DHS' role in advising, assisting, and ensuring that State and local governments develop and maintain national security and emergency preparedness telecommunications plans.

Name	Date	Description
Executive Order 12656, *Assignment of EP Responsibilities*	November 18, 1988	Delegates NS/EP responsibilities to Federal departments and agencies, instructs agencies to develop plans and capabilities that will ensure continuity of operations, and reaffirms the need for interagency cooperation in the pursuit of telecommunications NS/EP.
NCS Directive 3-1, *Telecommunications Operations*	August 10, 2000	Implements policy, assigns responsibilities, and establishes procedures for the Telecommunications Service Priority (TSP) Program. Authorizes priority services for domestic telecommunications services (e.g., Government Emergency Telecommunications Service [GETS] and Wireless Priority Service [WPS]).
Executive Order 13231, *Critical Infrastructure Protection*	October 16, 2001	Establishes the President's Critical Infrastructure Protection Board, tasked with ensuring the protection of information systems for critical infrastructure, including emergency preparedness communications and the physical assets that support these systems.
Homeland Security Presidential Directive (HSPD) 5, *Management of Domestic Incidents*	February 28, 2003	Directs the Secretary of DHS to develop and administer a national incident management system. The system is to provide a consistent nationwide approach to enable Federal, State, local, and tribal governments and the private sector to work together effectively and efficiently to prepare for, prevent, respond to, and recover from domestic incidents regardless of cause, size, or complexity.
HSPD 7, *Critical Infrastructure Identification, Prioritization, and Protection*	December 17, 2003	Calls for Federal departments and agencies to identify, prioritize, and coordinate the protection of critical infrastructures and key resources to prevent, deter, and mitigate the effects of deliberate efforts to destroy, incapacitate, or exploit them. Assigns DHS (delegated to the NCS) as the lead for coordinating protection of national critical infrastructures, including the communications sector.
HSPD 8, *National Preparedness*	December 17, 2003	Establishes policies to strengthen national preparedness to prevent and respond to terrorist attacks, major disasters, and other emergencies by requiring a national domestic all-hazards preparedness goal. Establishes mechanisms for improved delivery of Federal preparedness assistance to State and local governments, and outlines actions to strengthen the preparedness capabilities of Federal, State, regional, local, and tribal entities.
Spectrum Policy for the 21st Century, *The President's Spectrum Policy Initiative*	November 30, 2004	Establishes processes to implement a comprehensive U.S. Spectrum Policy to foster economic growth, ensure national and homeland security, maintain U.S. global leadership in communications technology development and services, and satisfy other vital needs in areas such as public safety, scientific research, Federal transportation infrastructure, and law enforcement. NTIA leads the implementation of this initiative. Also calls for DHS to develop a comprehensive plan for non-Federal public safety spectrum needs.
Executive Order 13407, *Public Warning System*	June 28, 2006	Calls for an effective, reliable, integrated, and flexible system to alert and warn the American people in all-hazard emergencies. DHS is the Executive Agent for the Public Alert and Warning System Program.
HSPD 20, *National Continuity Policy*	May 4, 2007	Establishes National Essential Functions, which prescribe continuity requirements for all executive departments and agencies and provide guidance for State, local, territorial, and tribal governments and private sector organizations.
NCS Directive 3-10, *Minimum Requirements for Continuity Communications Capabilities*	July 25, 2007	Requires that all departments and agencies that support National Essential Functions operate and maintain—or have dedicated access to—communications capabilities at their headquarters and alternate operating facilities, as well as mobile in-transit communications capabilities, to ensure continuation of mission critical functions across the full spectrum of hazards, threats, and emergencies, including catastrophic attacks or disasters.

A2.4 National-Level Policy and Planning Initiatives

Exhibit A2-5 describes the key national-level policy and planning initiatives that guide emergency response efforts.

Exhibit A2-5: Key National-Level Policy and Planning Initiatives

Name	Date	Description
National Incident Management System (NIMS)	March 1, 2004	The NIMS presents a unified approach to incident management, provides standard command and control structures, and emphasizes preparedness, mutual aid, and resource management. The NIMS emphasizes that establishing and maintaining a common operational picture and ensuring accessibility and interoperability are principal goals of communications and information management.
Manual of Regulations and Procedures for Federal Radio Frequency Management	May 2003 edition; September 2006 revision	Issued by the Assistant Secretary of Commerce for Communications and Information to address the Department of Commerce's frequency management responsibilities pursuant to delegated authority under Section 305 of the Communications Act of 1934, as amended.
National Infrastructure Protection Plan (NIPP)	July 2006	The NIPP, and supporting sector-specific plans, establishes a comprehensive risk management framework that provides the unifying structure for integrating existing and future critical infrastructure and key resource (CI/KR) protection efforts into a single national program. The NIPP specifies the key initiatives, milestones, and metrics required to protect the Nation's CI/KR and provides a coordinated approach that defines the roles and responsibilities of Federal, State, and local governments as well as the private sector.
National Preparedness Guidelines	September 2007	Provides readiness targets, priorities, standards for assessments and strategies, and a system for assessing the Nation's overall level of preparedness. Consists of related preparedness tools, such as the National Preparedness Vision, National Planning Scenarios, the Universal Task List, and the Target Capabilities List.
National Response Framework (NRF), including *Emergency Support Function (ESF) #2*	December 2004; re-released January 22, 2008	Establishes a comprehensive all-hazards approach to enhance the ability of the United States to manage domestic incidents. Provides the structure and mechanisms to coordinate and integrate incident management activities and emergency support functions across Federal, State, local, and tribal government entities, and the private sector. ESF #2, led by NCS, ensures Federal communications support to Federal, State, local, tribal, and private sector efforts.

A2.5 State, Regional, and Local Planning

Exhibit A2-6 describes some of the key regional, State, and local planning initiatives related to emergency communications.

Exhibit A2-6: Key Regional, State, and Local Planning Initiatives

Name	Date	Description
State and Local Guide (SLG) 101: Guide for All-Hazard Emergency Operations Planning	September 1996	Provides emergency response agencies with information on FEMA's concept for developing risk-based, all-hazard emergency operations plans. Clarifies the preparedness, response, and short-term recovery planning elements that warrant inclusion in State and local Emergency Operations Plans.
Tactical Interoperable Communications Plan (TICP)	December 2006	TICPs present a region's plan for establishing and maintaining tactical interoperable communications, defined as the rapid provision of on-scene, incident-based, mission-critical voice communications among all first-responder agencies, in support of an incident command system as defined in the NIMS model. Developed initially by the Urban Area Security Initiative (UASI) areas in response to Fiscal Year (FY) 2005 Homeland Security Grant Program (HSGP) guidance.
Statewide Communication Interoperability Plan (SCIP)	March 2008	Describes the strategic vision, goals, and key long-term and short-term strategic initiatives for States to improve communications interoperability. Serves as a mechanism and roadmap to align emergency responders at all levels of State government to improve communications interoperability. Developed initially in response to FY07 HSGP and Public Safety Interoperable Communications (PSIC) Grant Program requirements.

Appendix 3: Key Federal Emergency Communications Initiatives, Programs, Systems, and Services

This appendix presents a summary of key Federal initiatives related to emergency communications collected as part of the ECPC clearinghouse *Federal Interoperability Catalog*. While this is not an exhaustive inventory of Federal programs, the information below represents the most comprehensive data set to date and will act as living document. The summary below promotes emergency interoperable communications information sharing and awareness among Federal agencies by highlighting programs and initiatives that are related to other departments and agencies, including:

- Policy and Planning Initiatives
- Federal Systems and Services
- Information Sharing and Command and Control Centers
- Standards and Research, Development, Testing, and Evaluation (RDT&E) Initiatives
- Grant Funding Initiatives
- Training and Exercise Initiatives.

Exhibit A3-1 summarizes key emergency communications policy and planning initiatives.

Exhibit A3-1: Key Emergency Communications Policy and Planning Initiatives

Type of Policy/Plan	Key Policies, Plans, and Assessments	Lead Agency
Strategy, Legislation, Directives	▪ See Appendix 2 for overview of National Strategies, Legislation, Directives, and Executive Orders related to emergency communications	▪ Executive branch, Congress

Regulatory, Spectrum Management	▪ Regulation of interstate and international communications (by radio, television, wire, satellite, and cable)
	  – Spectrum (e.g., 700 MHz D Block, digital television transition, 800MHz rebanding)
	  – Alert and warning (e.g., Public Safety Access Point [PSAP], Enhanced 911, Emergency Alert System [EAS], commercial mobile alerts)
	  – Other (e.g., priority telecommunications and amateur radio services, special temporary authority)
		▪ FCC

	▪ Federal government spectrum management, communications policy initiatives	▪ NTIA
National Preparedness Doctrine[32]	▪ National Response Framework (NRF), Emergency Support Function #2 (ESF#2), National Incident Management System (NIMS)	▪ DHS
	▪ National Preparedness Guidelines: Target Capabilities List (TCL), Universal Task List (UTL), National Planning Scenarios	▪ DHS
Emergency Communications Planning	▪ National/regional planning: National Infrastructure Protection Plan (NIPP), National Emergency Communications Plan (NECP), FEMA Disaster Emergency Communications (DEC) planning, Regional Emergency Communications Coordination (RECC planning)	▪ DHS
	▪ State-level planning: Statewide Communication Interoperability Plans (SCIP), all-hazard emergency operations planning (and communications annexes)	▪ State agencies
	▪ Local-level planning: Tactical Interoperable Communications Plans (TICP), all-hazard emergency operations planning (and communications annexes)	▪ Local agencies
National-Level Assessments	▪ National Communications Capability Report (NCCR), SAFECOM National Interoperability Baseline Survey, DHS Nationwide Plan Review, Tactical Interoperable Communications Scorecard Report, others	▪ DHS
	▪ NSTAC Emergency Communications and Interoperability Report, Katrina After Action Reports, 9/11 Commission Reports	▪ Multiple authors

---

[32] Appendix 2 provides additional information on National Preparedness Doctrine.

Exhibit A3-2 presents key tactical and emergency communications systems and programs, as well as telecommunications and other support services provided by Federal government agencies.

Exhibit A3-2: Federal Tactical and Emergency Communications Systems and Services

Department	Agency/Bureau	Key Programs/Projects/Resources
Commerce	NTIA	Office of Spectrum Management (e.g., national interoperability channel resources)
DHS	Customs and Border Protection (CBP)	Secure Border Initiative Network (SBINet) Tactical Modernization Program
	Federal Emergency Management Agency (FEMA)	Disaster Emergency Communications (DEC) Mobile Emergency Response System (MERS) FEMA National Radio System (FNARS) Emergency Alert System (EAS) (with FCC, National Oceanic and Atmospheric Administration [NOAA]), Digital Emergency Alert System (DEAS) Geo-Targeted Alerting System (GTAS) (with NOAA) DHS Web Alert and Relay Network (WARN) Integrated Public Alert & Warning System (IPAWS) (with FCC, NOAA/NWS) National Warning and Alert System (NAWAS) Homeland Security Preparedness Technical Assistance Program (e.g., Response/Recovery focusing on Interoperable Communications)
	Immigrations and Customs Enforcement (ICE)	Atlas Program
	National Communications System (NCS)	Government Emergency Telecommunications Service (GETS) Telecommunications Service Priority (TSP) Program Wireless Priority Service (WPS) Shared Resources (SHARES) High-Frequency (HF) Radio Program ESF #2 Communications Asset Database (CAD)
	OEC	Integrated Wireless Network (IWN) Interoperable Communications Technical Assistance Program (ICTAP) SAFECOM (guidance, tools, templates) FPIC integration projects Communications Asset Survey and Mapping (CASM) Tool ECPC clearinghouse
	OIC	SAFECOM (R&D, T&E, Standards)
	Office of the Chief Information Officer (OCIO)	OneNet Homeland Security Information Network (HSIN)
	U.S. Coast Guard (USCG)	Rescue 21 Nationwide Automatic Identification System (NAIS) Deepwater
DoD	DoD	Single Channel Ground and Airborne Radio System (SINCGARS) Joint Tactical Radio System Transformational Satellite Communications System (TSAT) Joint task force civil support assets for disaster relief Global Information Grid (GIG)
	Department of the Army	Army installation land mobile radio (LMR) systems Joint Interoperability Test Command
	U.S. Marine Corps	Marine Corps Network Operations and Security Center
	Department of the Navy	National Enterprise Land Mobile Radio (ELMR) infrastructure
	National Guard Bureau (NGB)	Air National Guard (ANG)–Theater Deployable Communications (TDC) Joint Incident Site Communications Capability (JISCC) Army National Guard (ARNG) Joint Network Node (JNN) / Warfighter Information Network-Tactical (WIN-T)
DOJ	Wireless Management Office (WMO)	IWN DOJ 25 cities COMMTECH
	WMO/Federal Bureau of Investigation (FBI)	Satellite Mutual Aid Radio Talkgroup (SMART)
DOE	OCIO	Information Resource Program (includes wireless communications)
DOI	DOI OCIO Enterprise Infrastructure Division	Public Safety Communications Program

Department	Agency/Bureau	Key Programs/Projects/Resources
	Bureau of Land Management (BML)	National Interagency Fire Center (NIFC) assets
	Aircraft Management Division (AMD)	Joint aircraft all-risk-management, with USDA
DOT	National Highway Traffic Safety Administration	Enhanced 9-1-1 Next-Generation 9-1-1
USDA	U.S. Forest Service	National Interagency Incident Communications Division (NIICD) (partnership with Department of the Interior agencies)
Treasury	Wireless Programs Office	IWN
FCC	Public Safety Homeland Security Bureau (PSHSB)	PSHSB clearinghouse, ESF #2 CAD Disaster Information Reporting System (DIRS) Network Outage Reporting System (NORS)
NOAA	National Weather Service (NWS)	Alert and warning systems (e.g., EAS, GTAS)

Exhibit A3-3 presents examples of key homeland defense, homeland security, and public safety centers that have been established to share critical and sensitive information to protect the Nation, and to provide proper levels of command and control over field forces that could be brought to bear for incidents that require Federal assistance. These centers coordinate information, provide support to Federal, State, local, and tribal agencies engaged in response or recovery activities, and ensure that affected parties receive critical or sensitive information in a timely manner.

Exhibit A3-3: Information Sharing and Command and Control Centers

Coordination Centers	Lead Agency	Supporting/Participating Departments and Agencies
National Operations Center (NOC)	DHS/Office of Operations Coordination	Bureau of Alcohol, Tobacco, Firearms, and Explosives (ATF), Central Intelligence Agency (CIA), USCG, Bureau CBP, Defense Intelligence Agency (DIA), DoD, DOE, Department of Health and Human Services (HHS), DOI, Department of State, DOT, Department of Veterans Affairs (VA), Drug Enforcement Administration (DEA), Environmental Protection Agency (EPA), Federal Air Marshal Service (FAMS), FBI, FEMA, Federal Protective Service (FPS), Geo-spatial Mapping Office, ICE, Information Analysis Office, Infrastructure Protection Office, National Geospatial-Intelligence Agency (NGA), National Capital Region (NCR), NOAA, National Security Agency, Postal Inspection Service, DHS Public Affairs, DHS Science and Technology Directorate, United States Secret Service (USSS), DHS State and Local Coordination Office, Transportation Security Administration (TSA), Los Angeles Police Department (LAPD), Metropolitan Police of the District of Columbia (MPDC), New York Police Department (NYPD)
National Response Coordination Center (NRCC)	DHS/FEMA	Commerce, DoD, DOE, Department of Housing and Urban Development, DOI, DOJ, Department of Labor, Department of State, DOT, EPA, FCC, FEMA, General Services Administration, HHS, National Aeronautics and Space Administration, NCS, National Voluntary Organizations Active in Disaster, Nuclear Regulatory Commission, Office of Personnel Management, Social Security Administration, Treasury, U.S. Agency for International Development, U.S. Army Corps of Engineers, USCG, USDA, U.S. Postal Service, VA, American Red Cross, Corporation for National and Community Service, Small Business Administration, Tennessee Valley Authority
National Response Center (NRC)	DHS/USCG	Space and Naval Warfare Systems Command (SPAWAR), DoD/Edgewood Chemical Biological Center (ECBC), DOE, EPA, FBI, FEMA, HHS/Centers for Disease Control and Prevention (CDC), DOT/Federal Railroad Administration (FRA), National Transportation Safety Board (NTSB), Nuclear Regulatory Commission
National Interagency Fire Center (NIFC)	Interior/USFS	USFS/BLM, Bureau of Indian Affairs, Fish and Wildlife Service, National Park Service, NOAA/NWS, DOI/National Business Center/Aviation Management Division, US Fire Administration, National Association of State Foresters

A – 13

Coordination Centers	Lead Agency	Supporting/Participating Departments and Agencies
National Law Enforcement Communications Center (NLECC)	DHS/CBP	ICE
National Coordinating Center for Telecommunications (NCC)	DHS/NCS	Communications Information Sharing and Analysis Center (Comm ISAC)
National Counterterrorism Center (NCTC)	Director of National Intelligence	CIA, FBI, and 14 other classified and unclassified agencies
National Military Command Center (NMCC)	DoD	Joint Staff of the armed forces

Exhibit A3-4 presents key standards and RDT&E initiatives involving emergency communications.

Exhibit A3-4: Standards Development and RDT&E Initiatives

Type of Initiative	Initiative	Key Organizations/Departments/ Agencies
Digital Public Safety Radio Standards	APCO Project 25 (P25), P25 Compliance Assessment Program	APCO, Telecommunications Industry Association (TIA), DHS, National Institute of Standards and Technology (NIST)
Broadband Committees	APCO Project 25 Interface Committee (APIC) Broadband Task Group, Project Mesa, P34	APCO, TIA, NIST
Data Exchange Standards	Emergency Data Exchange Language (EDXL) Messaging Standards Initiative, Common Alerting Protocol (CAP)–Distribution Element (DE), Hospital Availability Exchange (HAVE) and Resource Messaging (RM), National Information Exchange Model (NIEM)	DOJ, DHS, COMCARE
RDT&E Programs	• DHS Science and Technology Directorate (S&T): 4.9 GHz Wireless Standard, Voice over Internet Protocol (VOIP) specifications, Digital Vocoder Working Group, Radio over Wireless Broadband (ROW-B), Multi-Band Radio • NTIA Institute for Telecommunications Sciences (ITS): Broadband Wireless, Digital LMR, IT, Propagation Measurements and Models, Spectrum Research, Technology Transfer • National Law Enforcement and Corrections Technology Center (NLECTC) System • Cooperative Research and Development Agreements (CRADA) • DoD RDT&E programs	▪ DHS/OIC ▪ ITS ▪ DOJ/National Institute of Justice (NIJ) ▪ DoC/NTIA, NIST ▪ DoD

Exhibit A3-5 presents key Federal grant initiatives related to interoperable and emergency communications.

Exhibit A3-5: Federal Grant Initiatives for Emergency Communications

Type of Initiative	Grant Program	Lead Agency
Interoperability Grant Programs	▪ Public Safety Interoperable Communications (PSIC) Grant Program ▪ Interoperable Emergency Communications Grant Program (IECGP)	NTIA DHS

National Preparedness Grant Programs (scope includes interoperable communications)	▪ Homeland Security Grant Program (HSGP)
	  – State Homeland Security Program (SHSP)
	  – Urban Area Security Initiative (UASI)
	  – Citizen Corps Program (CCP)
	  – Metropolitan Medical Response System (MMRS)
	▪ Law Enforcement Terrorism Prevention Program (LETPP)
	▪ Emergency Management Performance Grant (EMPG)
	▪ Assistance to Firefighters Grants (AFG)
	▪ Buffer Zone Protection Plan (BZPP)
	▪ Transit Security Grant Program (TSGP)
	▪ Homeland Security National Training Program (HSNTP) and Competitive Training Grant Program (CTGP)
		DHS

Grant Guidance, Tools, and Assistance	▪ Grant guidance materials and associated support
	  – SAFECOM grant guidance
	  – Authorized Equipment List (AEL)
	  – SAVER Program
	  –Technical assistance
	▪ InterAgency Board (IAB), Standardized Equipment List (SEL)
		DHS
		
		DOJ, DoD, cross-governmental participants

Exhibit A3-6 presents key Federal training and exercise initiatives involving emergency communications.

Exhibit A3-6: Federal Training and Exercise Initiatives

Type of Initiative	Key Program(s)	Lead Agency
Training	Emergency Management Institute (EMI) (e.g., residential courses, independent study [e.g., NIMS, NRF], continuity of operations)	DHS
	Communications Unit Leader (COML) curriculum development	DHS/OIC, Incident Management Systems Integration Division (IMSID), National Wildfire Coordinating Group (NWCG), FEMA
Exercise	National Exercise Program (NEP)	DHS/FEMA
	Homeland Security Exercise and Evaluation Program (HSEEP)	DHS
	Top officials (TOPOFF) 4	DHS/FEMA
	Determined accord	DHS/FEMA
	National Nuclear Security Formal Exercise Program	DOE/National Nuclear Security Administration (NNSA)
	Disaster response exercises (international and national exercises)	Federal Aviation Administration (FAA)
	Hurricane preparedness tabletop exercises	DHS
	Golden Phoenix	DoD
	TICP exercises	Requirement by DHS for UASI regions

Appendix 4: DHS Organizations with Responsibilities and Programs Supporting Emergency Communications

Improving the Nation's ability to communicate effectively during emergency situations is among the most fundamental missions assigned to DHS. With passage of the *Homeland Security Act of 2002* and subsequent amendments over the last five years, DHS has assumed lead responsibility for many of the U.S. Government's most important national communications functions, while simultaneously creating new programs to meet emerging communications needs at the Federal, State, local, and tribal levels.

The consolidation of emergency communications missions, roles, and responsibilities under DHS is an important step toward coordinating and improving communications planning, preparedness, protection, crisis management, and recovery operations after September 11, 2001. DHS' communications initiatives and capabilities serve a diverse set of customers: the President; the executive branch of the Federal Government; defense and intelligence agencies; law enforcement; State, local, and tribal authorities; emergency responders; and critical infrastructure owners and operators.

For the emergency response community, OEC was established in 2007 as the focal point for developing, implementing, and coordinating interoperable and operable communications for emergency responders at all levels of government. OEC oversees three programs for improving emergency communications for Federal, State, local, and tribal agencies—the Integrated Wireless Network (IWN), the Interoperable Communications Technical Assistance Program (ICTAP), and the SAFECOM program (excluding its RDT&E and standards functions). In addition, OEC is responsible for implementing new programs and initiatives to enhance interoperable communications, including:

- **Statewide Communication Interoperability Plans (SCIP):** SCIPs are locally driven, multi-jurisdictional, and multi-disciplinary plans to address statewide interoperability. For the first time in history, all 56 States and territories have developed SCIPs, marking a critical milestone in breaking down the barriers of the past and establishing a roadmap for future interoperability. These plans address designated critical elements for statewide interoperability and must be approved by OEC for a State to qualify for grant funding through the Homeland Security Grant Program and Public Safety Interoperable Communications (PSIC) Grant Program.

  > OEC's **Communications Assets Survey and Mapping (CASM)** tool provides an inventory and analysis of interoperability communications planning for use by emergency response agencies nationwide. The tool allows agencies to store and display data about their communications assets.

- **National Communications Capabilities Report (NCCR):** The NCCR provides a framework for evaluating current emergency communications capabilities across all levels of government. The NCCR will help government officials to determine priorities and to allocate resources more effectively.

- **Emergency Communications Preparedness Center (ECPC):** The ECPC is the Federal focal point and clearinghouse for coordinating interoperability efforts among Federal departments and agencies. OEC currently chairs the ECPC Working Group, which coordinated Federal input to the NECP. The ECPC's annual strategic assessment for Congress describes the current status of Federal interoperable communications.

To accomplish its overall mission, OEC must coordinate with other DHS organizations that have responsibilities for ensuring communications and with other Federal departments and agencies. The following describes OEC's primary partners within DHS, including their key communications functions, programs, and responsibilities.

FEMA Disaster Emergency Communications (DEC) Division, organized under FEMA's Disaster Operations Directorate, prepares for and delivers emergency communications assistance during major disasters. FEMA DEC plays a key role in integrating and coordinating Federal disaster communications services and capabilities in FEMA regions and in the incident area. Key FEMA DEC planning activities include the following:

- **State Emergency Planning:** To support FEMA's integration role, FEMA DEC assists in the development of emergency communications plans and procedures for regions and States; supports standards and technical advancements to improve communications; and conducts training, tests, and exercises of emergency communications capabilities and procedures. FEMA DEC also provides an integration and coordination point for Federal departments and agencies that provide disaster communications capabilities and support during incidents.

- **DEC Integration Branch:** The primary responsibilities of FEMA's Communications Integration Branch (CIB) is to advance the establishment of the DEC end-state architecture and integrate FEMA DEC services with FEMA Headquarters (HQ), regions, emergency communications program offices (e.g., OEC, OIC), communications capability providers (e.g., United States Coast Guard, National Guard Bureau, USNORTHCOM), and response agencies. The CIB supports the FEMA regional offices by providing assistance and guidance in DEC planning and policies, guidance and oversight of the RECCWGs, and assistance in a disaster when the region requires such assistance.

- **DEC Tactical Branch:** The Tactical Emergency Communications Branch (TECB) of the FEMA DEC Division is composed of two key components: Mobile Emergency Response Support (MERS) Program Management and MERS Detachments. MERS provides rapidly deployable command, control, and disaster emergency communications capabilities and tactical operations and logistics support for on-scene management of disaster response activities. MERS is a key FEMA disaster response asset that plays an important role in supporting disaster response operations

The **National Communications System** (NCS) is an interagency system that brings together 24 Federal departments and agencies in a joint planning framework for National Security and Emergency Preparedness (NS/EP) telecommunications. The NCS supports the Executive Office of the President for Enduring Constitutional Government, Continuity of Operations (COOP), and Continuity of Government (COG), and delivers a suite of priority telecommunications services to national leaders. To ensure effective planning and response, the NCS manages the National Coordinating Center for Telecommunications (NCC), a public-private partnership for sharing information and coordinating response and recovery operations.

The NCS has a number of responsibilities and programs to enhance communications for the emergency response community. As the coordinator for Emergency Support Function (ESF) #2 (Communications), the NCS is responsible for ensuring that the Nation's communications infrastructure and capabilities are maintained in any emergency situation. The NCS is responsible for coordinating the planning and provisioning of

> The NCS **SHAred RESources (SHARES) High-Frequency (HF) Radio Program** provides a single interagency emergency voice and data message-handling system. SHARES brings together the assets of thousands of HF radio stations to transmit NS/EP information when normal communications are unavailable. SHARES provides the Federal government with a forum for addressing issues affecting HF radio interoperability.

NS/EP communications for the Federal Government under all hazards, including crisis recovery and reconstitution. The NCS monitors emergency situations to determine the potential impact on existing telecommunications services and to ensure that sufficient telecommunications capability is provided to support response efforts.

The NCS also offers an array of NS/EP priority communications services and programs to support emergency response. The Government Emergency Telecommunications Service (GETS) provides emergency access and priority processing on the local and long-distance portions of the Public Switched Telephone Network (PSTN). The Wireless Priority Service (WPS) gives Federal, State, local, and critical infrastructure personnel priority access calling on cellular networks for NS/EP purposes during times of high network congestion. The Telecommunications Service Priority (TSP) Program managed by NCS gives NS/EP users priority processing of their telecommunications service requests in the event of service disruption.

The **Office for Interoperability and Compatibility** (OIC) was established in 2004 to strengthen and integrate interoperability and compatibility efforts to improve Federal, State, local, and tribal emergency response and preparedness. Managed by the Science and Technology Directorate, OIC helps coordinate interoperability issues across DHS. OIC programs and initiatives address critical interoperability and compatibility issues. Priority areas include communications, equipment, and training. Key OIC activities include:

- **Standards Acceleration:** OIC is working with NIST and the Institute for Telecommunication Sciences (ITS) to support the efforts of the emergency response community and the private sector, as they accelerate the development of the Project 25 (P25) suite of standards. P25 standards will help produce voice communications equipment that is interoperable and compatible, regardless of manufacturer. In addition to interoperability, P25 aims to promote spectral efficiency, backwards compatibility, and scalability. OIC is also partnering with emergency responders, Federal agencies, and standards development organizations, including the Organization for the Advancement of Structured Information Standards (OASIS), to accelerate the creation of data messaging standards. The EDXL Messaging Standards Initiative is a practitioner-driven, public-private partnership to create information sharing capabilities between disparate emergency response software applications, systems, and devices. The resulting Extensible Markup Language (XML) standards assist the emergency response community in sharing data seamlessly and securely while responding to an incident.

- **Compliance Assessment:** In collaboration with its partners, OIC is establishing a P25 Compliance Assessment Program (CAP) to provide demonstrable evidence of P25 product compliance. P25 CAP will improve adoption of P25 standards in manufacturer systems while creating a mechanism enabling procurement officers and the emergency response community to confidently purchase and use P25 compliant products. The P25 CAP program ensures that emergency response equipment is compliant, thus improving interoperable communications. It also stimulates competition among manufacturers, which results in more affordable technologies for the emergency response community.

- **Technology Demonstrations:** OIC conducts Technology Demonstration Projects across the Nation to test and demonstrate technologies in real-world environments, including data and video, and strategically assess results.

- **Communications Unit Leader (COML) Training:** OIC developed the COML curriculum to establish a standardized course of training for communications in a Type III incident. The Type III COML course trains emergency responders on how to be radio communications leaders during all-hazards emergency operations—significantly improving communications across multiple jurisdictions and disciplines responding to an incident. The course was delivered to the National Incident Management System (NIMS) Incident Management Systems Integration Division (IMSID) and was accepted as NIMS compliant. Through the development of the Type III COML course, DHS will provide a tool for training communications unit leaders and their command and general staff to perform the critical mission of managing interagency and cross-disciplinary communications during all-hazards incidents.

OEC and **U.S. Customs and Border Protection** (CBP) are collaborating on a series of communications projects to improve interoperability for law enforcement and other first responders along the Canadian and Mexican borders. CBP operates and maintains various command, control, communications, and intelligence (C3I) assets that could be used during a crisis. These include very high frequency (VHF) and high frequency (HF) national tactical radio networks and several local communications centers.

> The Secure Border Initiative (SBI) is a project to control U.S. borders and reduce illegal immigration. The **SBINet** is a key piece of SBI that promotes real-time communications among Border Patrol agents. Systems such as the Treasury Enforcement Communications System are also used to coordinate between CBP's Office of Border Patrol and ICE's Office of Investigations.

During all crises, **U.S. Bureau of Immigration and Customs Enforcement** (ICE) uses many public and government-operated systems to communicate with other executive branch agencies, elements of the Intelligence Community, and Federal, State, and local law enforcement agencies. In an effort to improve coordination and interoperability between CBP and ICE, DHS established the Secure Border Initiative (SBI) to link a number of organizational components with communications and other technology for a comprehensive border enforcement approach.

The **U.S. Coast Guard** maintains a disciplined command and control (C2) communications system that consists of several integrated components that are designed to be interoperable with DoD components in times of national emergency and/or war. The U.S. Coast Guard plays an active role in Federal interoperability forums, including the ECPC and Federal Partnership for Interoperable Communications (FPIC).

Appendix 5: The SAFECOM Interoperability Continuum

The SAFECOM Interoperability Continuum, developed with practitioner input from the DHS' SAFECOM program, is designed to help emergency response agencies and policymakers plan and implement interoperability solutions for data and voice communications. The tool identifies five critical elements that must be addressed to achieve a sophisticated interoperability solution: governance, standard operating procedures (SOP), technology, training and exercises, and usage of interoperable communications. Jurisdictions across the Nation can use the SAFECOM Interoperability Continuum to track their progress in strengthening interoperable communications.

Exhibit A5-1: SAFECOM Interoperability Continuum

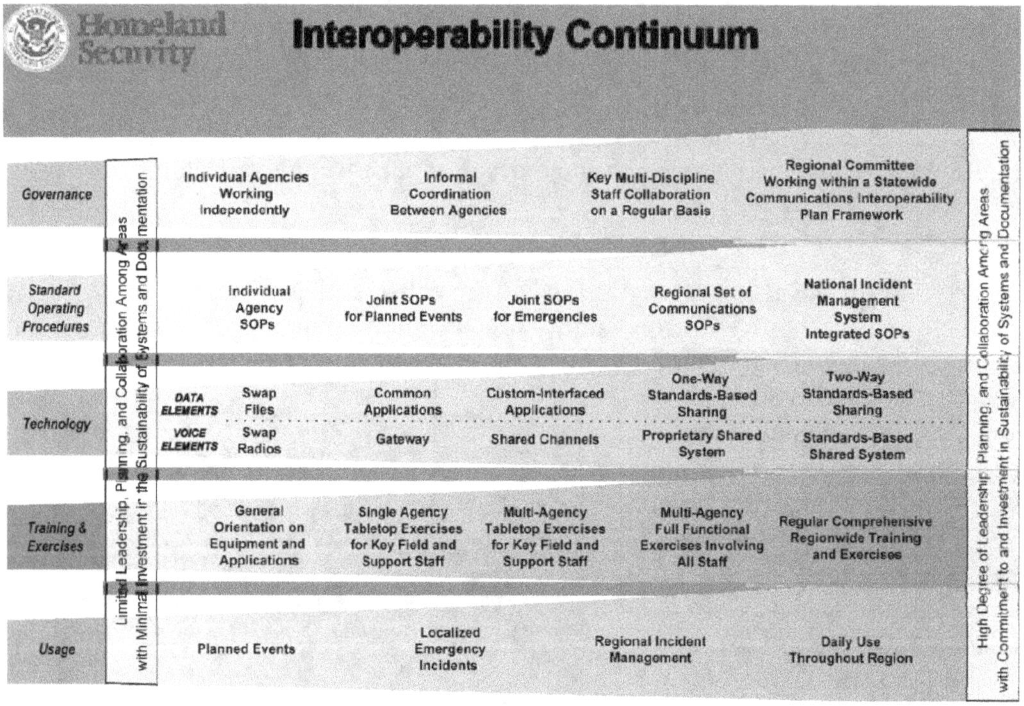

SAFECOM Interoperability Continuum Elements
Interoperability is a multidimensional challenge. To gain a true picture of a jurisdiction's interoperability capabilities, its progress in each of the five interdependent elements must be considered. For example, when a jurisdiction procures new equipment, it also should plan and conduct training and exercises to ensure that it make the best use of the equipment. What constitutes optimal interoperability is determined by the individual needs of an agency or jurisdiction. The SAFECOM Interoperability Continuum is a guide for jurisdictions when they are considering new interoperability solution, either because their needs have changed or because additional funding has become available. An evolving tool, the SAFECOM Interoperability Continuum supports the *National Preparedness Strategy* and aligns with national frameworks, including, but not limited to, the National Response Framework, NIMS, the National Emergency Communications Plan, and the National Communications Baseline Assessment. To maximize the SAFECOM Interoperability Continuum's value to the emergency response community, SAFECOM will regularly update the tool using a consensus process that involves practitioners, technical experts, and representatives from Federal, State, local, and tribal agencies.

Appendix 6: NECP Stakeholder Coordination

OEC, used a three-phased approach to develop the NECP that relied on stakeholder involvement at each stage: Data Gathering and Analysis, Strategy Development, and Plan Development and Review. See Exhibit A9-1.

Exhibit A6-1: National Emergency Communications Plan Approach

Stakeholder Outreach and Coordination

OEC considered stakeholder involvement the single most important element in the NECP development process. In accordance with Title XVIII requirements, OEC was directed to develop the NECP in cooperation with Federal departments and agencies; State, local, and tribal governments; emergency response providers; and the private sector. To engage this diverse group of stakeholders, OEC established a cross-governmental focus group of emergency response personnel and coordinated with existing councils, committees, associations, and partnerships that represent the emergency response community.

At the Federal level, OEC coordinated with the Emergency Communications Preparedness Center (ECPC) and the Federal Partnership for Interoperable Communications (FPIC). At the State and local levels, OEC worked closely with the SAFECOM Executive Committee/Emergency Response Council (EC/ERC) and the National Public Safety Telecommunications Council (NPSTC). Private sector involvement was coordinated through the Critical Infrastructure Partnership Advisory Council (CIPAC), which included representatives from the Communications Sector Coordinating Council, the Emergency Services Coordinating Council, the Information Technology Coordination Council, and the State, Local, Territorial, and Tribal Government Coordinating Council.

Phase 1: Data Gathering and Analysis

As a key first phase in the development process, OEC drew heavily from a foundation of emergency communications documentation and initiatives. During this data gathering and analysis phase, OEC worked in coordination with stakeholders to identify key emergency communications policies, strategies, plans, and reports for consideration. OEC then analyzed findings, lessons learned, issues, gaps, priorities, and recommendations from numerous sources, including the NCCR; SCIPs; the *2006 National Interoperability Baseline Survey* and numerous after-action reports from September 11, 2001, Hurricane Katrina and other recent natural and man-made incidents. These source documents were key drivers for the NECP's assessment of the current state-of-emergency communications and also helped shape the NECP's strategic goals, objectives, and initiatives. A list of the key documentation used to develop the NECP is presented in Appendix 10.

Phase 2: Strategy Development

Next, OEC worked closely with stakeholders to develop the high-level strategy for the NECP. Building on the legislative requirements, OEC used information gleaned from the data gathering and analysis effort, as well as stakeholder involvement, to craft the NECP's overarching strategic goals and priority initiatives. OEC worked with key coordination bodies (e.g., EC/ERC, ECPC, and NECP Focus Group) to develop and prioritize the specific near- and long-term emergency communications actions needed to implement these initiatives.

Phase 3: Plan Development and Review

During the final phases of NECP development, OEC conducted extensive outreach efforts to ensure that both DHS and external public and private sector stakeholders had an opportunity to review the document. Exhibit A9-2 illustrates the key steps in the evolution of the NECP—the key inputs and the considerations that shaped its goals and initiatives—and also demonstrates how OEC will work with the emergency response community to use the plan as a framework to improve its communications planning and capabilities as well as overall coordination nationwide.

Exhibit A6-2: Key Steps in Evolution of the NECP

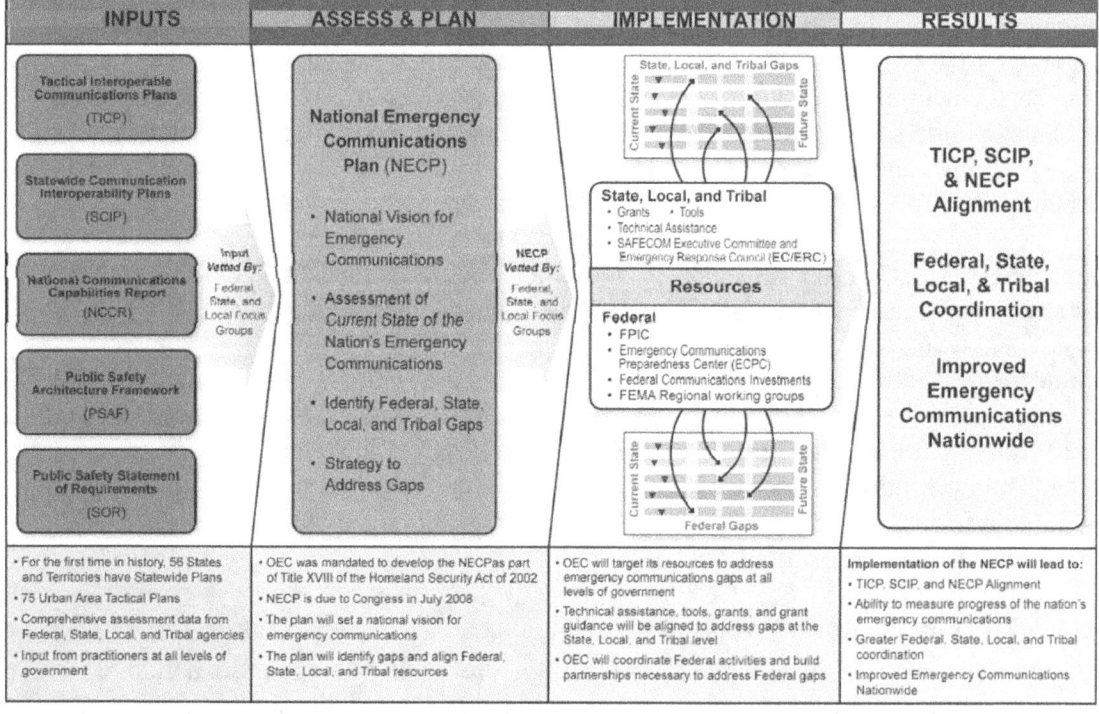

The success of the NECP requires the commitment of all emergency response disciplines at all levels of government. Achieving its goals and priority objectives will require coordination across geographical, political, and cultural jurisdictions and boundaries. OEC's current levers and incentives for driving NECP implementation include the provision of technical assistance to State, regional, local and tribal government officials; grant guidance and the coordination of DHS administered grant programs (such as the IECGP); and the coordination of Federal activities through the ECPC and FPIC. In addition, OEC will use statutory reporting requirements to monitor and report on progress towards implementing the NECP (e.g., State annual reports under the IECGP, the RECCWG annual reports, the ECPC annual strategic assessment, and OEC's assessment and biennial progress reports).

Appendix 7:   NECP Source Documents

State, Local, and Tribal

National Governors Association 2007 State Homeland Security Directors Survey. National Governors Association. December 2007.

Emergency Response Council Agreements on a Nationwide Plan for Interoperable Communications. SAFECOM Emergency Response Council (ERC) (with support from the Office of Emergency Communications and the Office for Interoperability and Compatibility). July 2007.

> *Public safety **interoperable communications topped the list of homeland security advisors' concerns in 2007**, as States continue to work to ensure that first responders from various agencies, jurisdictions, and levels of government can speak to each other during emergencies or at the scene of a disaster.*
> *Source: National Governors Association 2007 State Homeland Security Directors Survey*

Indian Country Border Security and Tribal Interoperability Pilot Program: The Importance of Tribes at the Frontlines of Border and Homeland Security (TBS Pilot Program) Final Report. The National Native American Law Enforcement Association; the National Congress of American Indians. March 2006.

National Associations, Task Forces, Advisory Committees, and Panels

Joint Advisory Committee on Communications Capabilities of Emergency Medical and Public Health Care Facilities Report to Congress. February 2008.

Association of Public-Safety Communications Officials-International (APCO) Homeland Security & Preparedness Version 2.1.
APCO International. September 2007.

National Security Telecommunications Advisory Committee Report on Emergency Communications and Interoperability. The President's National Security Telecommunications Advisory Committee. January 2007.

> *IP-based networks enable first responders to have the **flexibility and tools they need for effective response** and … modernize their existing radio networks so they work together with other existing and future communications networks and devices.*
> *Source: The Joint Advisory Committee on Communications Capabilities of Emergency Medical and Public Health Care Facilities, February 2008*

FCC Independent Panel Reviewing the Impact of Hurricane Katrina on Communications Networks. Federal Communications Commission Industry Panel. June 2006

Why Can't We Talk? National Task Force on Interoperability. February 2003.

Final Report of the Public Safety Wireless Advisory Committee to the Federal Communications Commission. September 1996.

Federal Government Reports, Assessments, Plans, and Strategies

Congress, White House, and Special Commissions

The National Strategy for Homeland Security. White House Homeland Security Council. October 2007.

The Final Report of the Select Bipartisan Committee to Investigate the Preparation for and Response to Hurricane Katrina. Select Bipartisan Committee to Investigate the Preparation for and Response to Hurricane Katrina, U.S. House of Representatives. February 2006.

The Federal Response to Hurricane Katrina: Lessons Learned. White House Homeland Security Advisor. February 2006.

The 9-11 Commission Report. The National Commission on Terrorist Attacks. July 2004.

> *The nation's emergency communications systems "must be resilient, either able to withstand destructive forces regardless of cause or sufficiently redundant to suffer damage and remain reliable.*
>
> *Source: The National Strategy for Homeland Security, revised October 2007*

> *Communications challenges across the Gulf Coast region in Hurricane Katrina's wake were more a problem of basic operability, than one of equipment or system interoperability.*
>
> *Source: Federal Response to Hurricane Katrina: Lessons Learned, February 2006*

The Department of Homeland Security

The National Communications Capabilities Report. Department of Homeland Security, Office of Emergency Communications. March 2008.

Target Capabilities List: A Companion to the National Preparedness Guideline. Department of Homeland Security. September 2007.

National Incident Management System (NIMS). Department of Homeland Security. August 2007.

The National Infrastructure Protection Plan (NIPP): Communications Sector Specific Plan. Department of Homeland Security, Office of Infrastructure Protection. May 2007.

The National Infrastructure Protection Plan: Emergency Services. Department of Homeland Security, Office of Infrastructure Protection. May 2007.

Tactical Interoperable Communications Scorecards Summary Report. Department of Homeland Security. January 2007.

Federal Emergency Management Agency (FEMA) Disaster Emergency Communications (DEC) Program Assessment. Department of Homeland Security, FEMA. January 2007.

SAFECOM 2006: National Interoperability Baseline Survey. Department of Homeland Security, SAFECOM Program. December 2006.

Answering the Call: Communication Lessons Learned from the Pentagon Attack. Department of Homeland Security, Public Safety Wireless Network (PSWN) Program. January 2002.

> **2006 SAFECOM Survey—**
> - 66% of public agencies use interoperability to some degree
> - Interoperability at local levels tends to be more advanced than between State and local agencies
>
> **TICP Scorecards—**
> - 68% of urban metro areas had established regional interoperability
> - 80% of urban/metro areas use shared systems and/or shared channels daily to provide interoperability

Appendix 8: Glossary of Terms

Agreements. Governance capability sub-element encompassing mechanisms approved to govern interagency coordination and the use of interoperable emergency communications solutions.

Continuity of Communications. Ability of emergency response agencies to maintain communications capabilities when primary infrastructure is damaged or destroyed.

Cross-Discipline. Involving emergency response providers from different disciplines (e.g., police, fire, EMS).

Cross-Jurisdiction. Involving emergency response providers from different jurisdictions (e.g., across State, county, or regional boundaries).

Decision-Making Groups. Governance capability sub-element that refers to a collection of public safety practitioners and leaders who pool their expertise to improve interoperable emergency communications.

Emergency Communications. Means and methods for transmitting and receiving information necessary for successful incident management, when needed and as authorized.

Exercises. Training and exercises capability sub-element encompassing emergency scenarios developed to establish proficiency in identifying communications resources needed and available, implementing processes and procedures, and leveraging solutions to effectively establish and maintain communications.

Funding. Governance capability sub-element encompassing the levels and reliability of financial resources available for one-time capital investments and recurring operating costs in support of interoperable emergency communications.

Frequency of Use and Familiarity. Usage capability sub-element encompassing the level of familiarity, proficiency, and frequency with which interoperable emergency communications solutions are activated and used.

Governance. Capability element that includes government leadership, decision-making groups, agreements, funding, and strategic planning.

Interoperability. Ability of emergency responders to communicate among jurisdictions, disciplines, frequency bands, and levels of government as needed and as authorized. System operability is required for system interoperability.

Jurisdiction. Geographical, political, or system boundary as defined by each State.

Leadership. Governance capability sub-element encompassing the involvement of government leaders and their commitment to ensuring the political and fiscal priority of interoperable emergency communications.

Operability. Ability of emergency responders to establish and sustain communications in support of mission operations.

Operability Assurance. Process of ensuring that emergency response providers and government officials can continue to communicate in the event of natural disasters, acts of terrorism, or other man-made disasters.

Policies, Practices, and Procedures. Standard operating procedures sub-element encompassing the range of formal and informal communications policies, practices, and procedures.

Private Sector Emergency Response Providers. Businesses and other nongovernmental organizations that provide emergency services in support of major incidents.

Response Level Emergency Communications. Capacity of individuals with primary operational leadership responsibility[33] to manage resources and make timely decisions during a multi-agency incident without technical or procedural communications impediments. In addition to communicating to first-level subordinates in the field, the Operations Section Chief should be able to communicate upwards to the incident command level[34] (e.g. between the Operations Section Chief and Incident Command). As the incident grows and transitions, Incident Command/Unified Command can move off scene and may require communication between Incident Command and off-scene EOCs, dispatch centers, and other support groups as appropriate.

Routine Incidents. Emergencies that happen on a regular basis. Examples of these types of events are further explained in the Usage element of the SAFECOM Interoperability Continuum as planned events, localized emergency incidents, regional incident management (interstate or intrastate), and daily use throughout the region.

Significant Incidents. Interoperability and continuity of communications are the emphasis for response-level emergency communications during significant events. *Homeland Security Presidential Directive 8: National Preparedness* (HSPD-8) sets forth 15 national planning scenarios that highlight a plausible range of significant events, such as terrorist attacks, major disasters, and other emergencies, that pose the greatest risk to the Nation. Any of these 15 scenarios should be considered when planning for a significant incident in which all major emergency communications infrastructure is destroyed.

Standard Operating Procedures. Capability element that includes the range of informal and formal policies, practices, and procedures that guide emergency responder interactions and the use of interoperable communications solutions.

Strategic Planning. Governance capability sub-element encompassing the disciplined efforts and processes to establish long-term goals and objectives for interoperable emergency communications.

System Functionality. Technology capability sub-element encompassing the range of fixed and mobile/deployable systems and equipment used for interoperable emergency communications and associated voice, data, and video capabilities.

---

[33] As defined in the National Incident Command System 200 - Unit 2 - Leadership and Management.

[34] As defined in the National Incident Management System, FEMA 501/Draft August 2007, p.47.

System Performance. Technology capability sub-element encompassing the availability, reliability, and scalability of communications systems and equipment.

Technology. Capability element that encompasses the systems and equipment that enable emergency responders to share information efficiently and securely during an emergency incident, and addresses the functionality, performance, interoperability, and continuity capabilities of those systems and equipment.

Training. Training and exercises capability sub-element encompassing the scope and frequency of educational activities related to interoperable emergency communications.

Training and Exercises. Capability element that includes educational activities and simulations conducted to help ensure that emergency responders know their roles and are properly prepared to respond to a wide range of emergencies.

Usage. Capability element that refers to the frequency and familiarity with which emergency responders use interoperable emergency communications solutions.

Appendix 9:   Acronyms

AEL	Authorized Equipment List
AES	Advanced Encryption Standard
AFG	Assistance to Firefighters Grants
APCO	Association of Public-Safety Communications Officials–International
APIC	APCO Project 25 Interface Committee
AVL	Automatic Vehicle Location
BBTG	APIC Broadband Task Group
BIA	Bureau of Indian Affairs
BORTAC	Border Tactical Communications
CAI	Common Air Interface
CAP	Common Alerting Protocol
CAP	Compliance Assessment Program
CASM	Communications Asset Survey and Mapping Tool
CBP	Customs and Border Protection
CCI	Command, Control and Interoperability
CCP	Citizen Corps Program
CDMA	Code Division Multiple Access
CFR	Code of Federal Regulations
CIPAC	Critical Infrastructure Partnership Advisory Council
COG	Continuity of Government
COML	Communications Unit Leader
COMT	Communications Unit Technicians
COOP	Continuity of Operations
COP	Committee of Principals
COPS	Community Oriented Policing Services
CTCSS	Continuous Tone Controlled Squelch System
DEC	Disaster Emergency Communications
DHS	Department of Homeland Security
DIRS	Disaster Information Reporting System
DM	Disaster Management
DoD	Department of Defense
DOE	Department of Energy
DOI	Department of the Interior
DOJ	Department of Justice

DOT	Department of Transportation
DSCA	Defense Support to Civil Authorities
EC/ERC	Executive Committee/Emergency Response Council (SAFECOM)
ECPC	Emergency Communications Preparedness Center
EDXL	Emergency Data Exchange Language
EMS	Emergency Medical Services
EMT	Emergency Medical Technician
EOC	Emergency Operations Center
ESF	Emergency Support Function
FAS	Frequency Assignment Subcommittee
FBI	Federal Bureau of Investigation
FCC	Federal Communications Commission
FCD	Federal Continuity Directive
FDMA	Frequency Division Multiple Access
FEMA	Federal Emergency Management Agency
FIPS	Federal Information Processing Standard
FLEWUG	Federal Law Enforcement Wireless Users Group
FM	Frequency Modulation
FPIC	Federal Partnership for Interoperable Communications
FY	Fiscal Year
G&T	Grants and Training
GETS	Government Emergency Telecommunications Service
GPS	Global Positioning System
GSM	Global System for Mobile Communications
HAZMAT	Hazardous Material
HF	High Frequency
HSEEP	Homeland Security Exercise and Evaluation Program
HSGP	Homeland Security Grant Program
HSPD	Homeland Security Presidential Directive
Hz	Hertz
ICC	Interoperable Communications Committee
ICE	Immigration and Customs Enforcement
ICP	Incident Command Post
ICS	Incident Command System
ICTAP	Interoperable Communications Technical Assistance Program
iDEN	Integrated Digital Enhanced Network

IECGP	Interoperable Emergency Communication Grant Program
IGA	Intergovernmental Agreement
IMSID	Incident Management Systems Integration Division
IP	Internet Protocol
IR	Incident Response
IRAC	Interdepartment Radio Advisory Committee
IT	Information Technology
IWN	Integrated Wireless Network
JISCC	Joint Incident Site Communications Capability
JITC	Joint Interoperability Test Command
JNN	Joint Network Nodes
JTRS	Joint Tactical Radio System
kHz	Kilohertz
LE	Law Enforcement
LEPC	Local Emergency Planning Committee
LETPP	Law Enforcement Terrorism Prevention Program
LMR	Land Mobile Radio
MAA	Mutual Aid Agreement
MERS	Mobile Emergency Response Support
MESA	Mobility for Emergency and Safety Applications
MHz	Megahertz
MMRS	Metropolitan Medical Response System
MOA	Memorandum of Agreement
MOU	Memorandum of Understanding
NAC	Network Access Code
NCC	National Coordinating Center for Telecommunications
NCCC	National Command and Coordination Capability
NCCR	National Communications Capabilities Report
NCR	National Capital Region
NCS	National Communications System
NCSD	National Communications System Directive
NECP	National Emergency Communications Plan
NERCS	National Emergency Responder Credentialing System
NGB	National Guard Bureau
NGO	Nongovernmental Organization
NIC	National Integration Center
NIEM	National Information Exchange Model

NIFOG	National Interoperability Field Operations Guide
NIJ	National Institute of Justice
NIMS	National Incident Management System
NIPP	National Infrastructure Protection Plan
NIST	National Institute of Standards and Technology
NORTHCOM	U.S. Northern Command
NPSPAC	National Public Safety Planning Advisory Committee
NPSTC	National Public Safety Telecommunications Council
NRF	National Response Framework
NRP	National Response Plan
NS/EP	National Security and Emergency Preparedness
NSTAC	National Security Telecommunications Advisory Committee
NTIA	National Telecommunications and Information Administration
NVOAD	National Voluntary Organizations Active in Disasters
O&M	Operations and Maintenance
OCIO	Office of the Chief Information Officer
OEC	Office of Emergency Communications
OGC	Office of General Counsel
OIC	Office for Interoperability and Compatibility
P25	Project 25
PDA	Personal Digital Assistant
PSAP	Public Safety Answering Point
PSIC	Public Safety Interoperable Communications Grant Program
PSWAC	Public Safety Wireless Advisory Committee
PSWN	Public Safety Wireless Network
PTT	Push-to-Talk
QoS	Quality of Service
R&D	Research and Development
RADO	Radio Operator
RDT&E	Research, Development, Testing, and Evaluation
RECCWG	Regional Emergency Communications Coordination Working Group
RF	Radio Frequency
RoIP	Radio over Internet Protocol
SBI	Secure Border Initiative
SCIP	Statewide Communication Interoperability Plan
SdoC	Supplier's Declaration of Compliance
SDR	Software Defined Radio

SEL	Standardized Equipment List
SHARES	Shared Resources Program
SHSP	State Homeland Security Program
SIEC	State Interoperability Executive Council
SME	Subject Matter Expert
SOP	Standard Operating Procedure
STR	Strategic Technology Reserve
SWAT	Special Weapons and Tactics
TCL	Target Capabilities List
TDMA	Time Division Multiple Access
TIA	Telecommunications Industry Association
TICP	Tactical Interoperable Communications Plan
TOPOFF	Top Officials
TSP	Telecommunications Service Priority
UA	Urban Areas
UASI	Urban Area Security Initiative
UCALL	UHF Calling Channel
UHF	Ultra High Frequency
ULS	Universal Licensing System
UPS	Uninterruptible Power Supply
USCG	United States Coast Guard
USDA	United States Department of Agriculture
USFS	United States Forest Service
UTAC	UHF Talk Around Channel
VCALL	VHF Calling Channel
VA	Department of Veteran Affairs
VHF	Very High Frequency
VoIP	Voice over Internet Protocol
VTAC	VHF Talk Around Channel
WIN-T	Warfighter Information Network - Tactical
WPS	Wireless Priority Service